FOREVER MORE

A Love Story from the Edge of Eternity

D1213497

Michele DeLuca

Joyride Press
Grand Island, NY
www.MicheleDeLuca.net

This is a work of fiction. Names, characters, places and incidents are products of the author's imagination and are used fictitiously and not to be construed as real. However, Lily Dale is an actual Spiritualist community in New York state. "Forever More: A Love Story at the Edge of Eternity," is inspired by the author's lifelong fascination with what comes after this life; and her wide collection of real life stories shared by those who have researched or experienced events similar to those that occur in the story.

ISBN 13: 9780692629215 Joyride Press

ISBN: 0692629211

TABLE OF CONTENTS

DEDICATION

This book is dedicated to my husband, Doug, and my sons, Douglas and Luke, for whom I written these words of hope and love. You have been my greatest gifts in this life.

To Tareya and Emily; I could not ask for two more beautiful and brilliant women to accompany my beloved sons on their journeys. Thank you for walking beside them.

To my mother and father, who taught me my earliest lessons about love, and my brothers, Jerry, Doug and Tom, who — along with me — are the evolution and expansion of everything our parents could give.

To the aunts, uncles and cousins in my great big Italian family, especially Denise, Donna, Cheryl, Paula, Sue and Darcy who have taught me the gifts of connection; and to my great big Greek family, who I have loved getting to know.

To my husband's siblings, Tom, Dave and Laura, and their families, who accepted me as one of their own, and whom I love as if they were.

To the Godmothers of this book, Mary O'Keefe, Kathy Kifer, Marilyn Timpanaro, and C.K. Brooke. After all these words, there are not enough to thank each of you.

To my nieces and nephews and their families: Mishayla, Maggie and Alex, Justin, Reed, Bailey and Grant; Ryan and Reggie; Jeff and Danny; Jimmo; Shannon, Ben, Kris, Kelly; Nick, Josh, Jamie and Matt; as well as Greg and Christine, Kim and Matthew; and Stephen and Danni. I am so proud of each of you and feel there is hope for the world because of you.

To all of the dearest friends who have walked beside me in my adult life, especially Cindy, who taught me about courage; Brandy, who taught me about redemption and Marcia who taught me about the strength of the human spirit. I am more because of each of you.

To my sister-in-law, Diane, who taught me the power of enduring love despite impossible challenge.

And to Casey, my best friend, who has walked this path with me since we were young. We have followed our dreams together and because of you, I have never felt alone. Thank you for being there, always.

PROLOGUE

As passings go, he told me his was a good one. When they found his body, there was a slight smile upon his face as if he were happily dreaming in his favorite armchair. It wasn't long after his earthly remains had been dispatched to the cemetery, that his spirit started showing up in my life. And while I know it sounds odd that anyone could fall in love with a dead man, I have to tell you that his energy was more alive than anyone I've ever known in physical form.

He often appeared to me dressed in the dapper style of the forties, which he told me was the best time of his former life. He'd wear a crisp white shirt tucked into the trim waist of his wide-leg pants, held up by a pair of suspenders. His hair was gleaming black and slicked back in unruly waves he would calm with a hand whenever he was trying to concentrate.

In the beginning, I thought he had come to me for help to heal the hearts of his daughter and granddaughter. Though that was part of it, he also saved my life and led me to finally understand what it felt like to be truly known and exquisitely loved. His presence helped to unfold in me an astounding late-life blossoming of which I couldn't have dreamt. Much later, when I was an old woman, I realized it was all of that and so much more. My name is Rebecca St. Claire, and this is my story of Sebastian.

1

Everything was ending the first day I saw him. It was the last day of school and the kids in my second grade class were especially unruly. I didn't blame them; I, too, was anxious to slip into the summer, set free from the relentless ticking of the big round clock that pushed me through my days, staring down from over the blackboard in the back of the room. I didn't have the resources in those final hours of the school year to deal with the chaos typically created by my high-spirited students. Ever since the chemotherapy, I tired much more easily and because of that I felt, from somewhere deep within, that I had not been lucky this round. Or perhaps it was that I didn't believe in luck anymore.

Maddy, a dark-eyed seven-year-old and a favorite of mine though I tried not to have them, had raised her hand and uttered the words every teacher dreads, "I think I'm going to be sick." And then she was, vomiting all over the picture book on her desk, which she had just taken out at my request so that I could collect them. I knew from my nearly thirty years of teaching that elementary students do not take well to the public emission of bodily fluids and mayhem erupted, cued by her cry of dismay. Some of the vomit had projected onto the back and hair of Celene, the little girl who sat in front of Maddy. Feeling the wetness, Celene started crying too and suddenly the whole class was reacting, with a few of the boys especially delighted by the unexpected diversion from our task-bound march toward summer vacation. In my post-chemo state, I was more vulnerable to smells and nearly sick myself at the acrid scent. But an elementary school teacher must remain calm during catastrophes large and small, so I began to restore order to my room.

"Maddy, it's going to be OK," I said, dabbing at her with the paper towel I always kept folded in my pocket for such events. I pointed to the little bathroom in the back of the classroom. "Go wash yourself off. I'll clean this up while you're gone." I gave the sniffling little girl a gentle push to get her moving and then turned to Celene. I wiped the tears from her sweet face and gave her a hug before returning my attention to the smelly mess, trying to breathe through my mouth so as not to make it worse.

It was then I had the unmistakable feeling there was another adult in the room. I thought perhaps someone had walked in while I was occupied with Maddy's upheaval, but I hadn't heard the door open. When I turned to see who was there, all I saw was a soft flash of light out of the corner of my eye, like a firefly blink. For a few seconds, I had the oddest sensation, as if someone was watching over the scene with amused sympathy. Then the moment passed and I went back to work, calming everyone and cleaning vomit.

Thankfully, the mess was wiped up quickly. An opened window and a couple squirts of air freshener made the room as good as new. My inclusion class, comprised of students of varying abilities, from high achievers to several special needs children with mental or physical disabilities, settled down and began gathering their things, preparing for the final moments of the last day of school. I shook my head to clear it and focused on ushering my young charges out the door. As I did so, I noticed Charlie, one of my students diagnosed with autism, sitting at his desk in the back of the room, staring at something and smiling. I was struck by how beautiful he looked, his auburn curls bobbing as he nodded his head in excitement. I hadn't seen him respond so enthusiastically to much of anything the entire year. His blue eyes were shining and engaged.

Charlie never spoke. He usually had an aide at his side to help him navigate his schoolwork, and she used a special notebook full of symbols, pictures, and words to help him stay calm and focused. I'd never even heard him make a noise beyond grunting, and often he would just sit at his desk and snap the green rubber band he wore on his wrist, an action that seemed to soothe him. Typically, his aide would try to gently turn him towards whatever activity the rest of the class was pursuing, but she had left the room to bring some of his paperwork to the main office, and he was alone.

Charlie laughed in delight, watching the spot where I'd seen the flash. I squinted at a barely perceptible shape of rippling energy. Though I was intimately familiar with people who believed that spirits and ghosts appeared out of nowhere, I was startled by what seemed to be an opaque human form standing near the boy's desk and even more shocked by Charlie's response. My young student was speaking quietly, his lips moving quickly while the human-like form seemed to listen and nod. Then, it lifted a hand and tenderly patted Charlie's shoulder before disappearing.

Charlie blinked several times and then began to cry softly, as if begging the apparition to return. I was about to comfort him when his aide hurried back into the room, eyes wide at the sight of his anguish. She quickly got out his notebook and flipped to images she knew would calm him. She pointed to a photo of children on the playground, which he especially liked, and talked to him quietly, saying the same soothing words over and over. "The playground is fun, Charlie. We're going to the playground today." Her words slowly lured his attention away from the unexpected visitor she hadn't seen.

I breathed a sigh of relief. Charlie was special in the purest sense of the word, and I felt very connected to him, so his pain hurt my heart. As I saw him snapping the rubber band on his wrist, I knew he had begun the process of self-comfort. I turned my attention to the rest of the class and our last goodbye. I would miss them all, especially Charlie, but in the past decades of my career, I had always been comforted knowing I would be able to watch them grow as they moved through the grades of my elementary school. They would be other teachers' students, but I felt a part of them would always belong to me, even the most challenging among them. The end-of-the-year had been easier when I knew I would be there for them if they needed me, but these last months had proved to me that no one is promised tomorrow. As I said goodbye to each of my students, hugging them one by one and whispering words of encouragement into their ears, I knew I might never see any of them again.

When Charlie's aide walked him to the door, I thanked her for her care and hard work helping him adapt in my class. Then I knelt down to eye level with Charlie. He looked away, but I spoke as if he were looking right at me. "It was a pleasure to have you in my class this year, Charlie. You are a wonderful young man, and you helped me teach the children that while our differences make us unique, we share much in common. I just wanted to thank you for that. I hope you have a wonderful life."

He looked over my shoulder at the spot where the apparition had appeared. A corner of his mouth turned up in a shadow of a smile. Our eyes met for an instant, and I saw a moment of clarity within his before they went blank once more. I was staring at him in surprise when his aide leaned over and said, "Come on, Charlie. Your mom is waiting."

They were the last to leave my room. I watched them walk away, suddenly aware that the preceding moments might have been my last as a teacher. I closed the door and leaned upon it to survey my empty classroom.

I could still feel the noisy imprint of each child's energy as silence seeped into my room. I shut my eyes and let it wash over me as I did every year. "I wish them happiness and peace," I whispered in a sort of prayer, in case there was some great and powerful being out there in the stratosphere watching over all children, but I wasn't hopeful. They were urban kids from poor neighborhoods, some challenged with physical, mental, and emotional difficulties.

If there was a God, he apparently didn't think being poor was hardship enough. I was certain that prayers alone couldn't keep my students safe, but there was never anything more that I could do than teach them as best I could and then send them on their way in the hope that somebody out there was watching over them.

As I looked around the empty room, I wondered about Charlie's visitor. I hadn't thought about spirits since I was a kid, when my mother and grandmother made their living talking to dead people. I had certainly never seen a spirit before.

I began to pick up the books the children had left on their desks. Last year, my cancer had brought me closer to the precipice of eternity than I had ever been before, and I'd spent the months since wondering about life and death. The two most important people in my life had believed that there was so much more to come when we die, but I'd never had any proof that their beliefs were anything more than wishful thinking. If anyone could have made their way back from the dead, my mother and my grandmother would surely have found a way to get back to me. If they, who were certain such things were possible, could so completely disappear, then how could the work to which they had devoted their lives be anything more than deluded fantasy?

But what had just happened in my classroom? I decided that it must have been a combination of my fuzzy post-chemo brain and the last-day-of-school commotion. I must have imagined the exchange between Charlie and the invisible presence. Perhaps our extraordinary connection as my student left was his extreme response to our parting. After all, we'd just spent the last nine months together. Either way, I had my hands full clearing out my classroom for what could be the last time.

I dropped the books on my desk and saw my cell phone blinking. It was a text from my husband, Michael. I frowned, and pressed a button on the phone so I could see his message. "We have to talk," it read.

Talk. That was almost funny. What the hell was there left to say?

2

My marriage was over, but Michael was a clever and successful defense attorney and believed he could argue his way out of anything. I knew he was planning, one more time, to try to change my mind. The text message he'd sent me that afternoon was the finale of a long and emotional series of conversations that had taken place over the past few weeks. I hadn't yet told him I suspected that the cancer that was once in my uterus had returned, despite the surgery and wearying round of chemotherapy and radiation I'd endured last summer.

As we sat together that night in our living room, Michael rehashed the whole dreadful story, which had begun last year between him and a younger co-worker. Apparently, she was his soul mate. Too. He loved us both he said. His face was pinched with regret as he brushed away tears with the back of his hand. "I would never deliberately try to hurt you, " he said. "I want you to stay. We can deal with this together."

I stared at him, resisting the impulse to grab my paper towel square and hand it to him as if he were one of my students.

As he continued his crazy argument for my staying in our home while he lived between two households, my eyes wandered over to our wedding photo on the desk. We had made such a lovely couple back then, him a lanky blonde in a white tuxedo, his sun streaked hair making him look like a cross between surfer dude and high school prom king; me standing next to him, the top of my head coming to just beneath his chin. My dark hair hung in waves around my shoulders, and I wore a simple white dress and a veil of Spanish lace. We were hippie children, full of hope and out to change the world. We worked together in the poorest neighborhoods of Cleveland. While I taught the children, he provided legal assistance to their families. It was not easy work, but the rewards satisfied him as much as they did me, and I was proud of both of us. Until now.

I pulled my attention back to the one-sided argument that was taking place in my living room where we were surrounded by the neatly arranged possessions from our life together: books, paintings and recycled furniture collected from thirty years of strolling hand-in-hand through flea markets and bartering at garage sales. Between the exhausting effects of the chemo on my body and my resolve to leave our marriage, it was hard to concentrate on Michael's carefully presented pitch to allow himself the best of both worlds, his mistress and his wife. I couldn't imagine a universe where my husband slept with another woman while I waited for him in our bed. Still, he persisted, delivering a passionate closing argument to explain why he was not willing to give up either of us. I tried to listen, sitting in my favorite overstuffed chair with the soft, green blanket we'd bought in Dublin wrapped around my shoulders, but his words were pinpricks in my heart.

Then, I saw it again. A spark of light at the edge of my line of sight seemed to briefly illuminate the darkest corner of the room. When I fixed my eyes upon it, it disappeared. I blinked and tried to return my attention to Michael. It might have been that my eyesight was faltering from the chemical residue in my system, but somehow I knew that spark was the same presence that had appeared in my classroom that day. The change in the energy of the room and the quickening of my heart felt exactly the same. Except this time, the movement was more distinct, the flicker more deliberate. When it disappeared, it was as if a light switched off. The corner of the room went dark.

The presence had been so bright that I looked to see if Michael had seen it too. But he was intent on making his case. "I was simply trying to give her some guidance, tell her how to get her life back together, when she reached out for me…"

He put his head down, ashamed. "She wanted more. And I wanted more, too. Before I knew it, we were lovers."

We'd had this conversation so many times lately that I had grown tired of the words. While a part of me would always feel love for him, it was not enough to consider the life he wanted to live. The emotional ties that had once bound us tightly had loosened over the years, and I wondered about the role I'd played in sending him into the arms of another woman. I didn't speak because I continued to feel the presence of another person in the room. It made me uncomfortable, as if we were discussing our most intimate secrets in front of a stranger. I stood up, hoping to end Michael's oratory, when my husband delivered the final blow.

"She's pregnant," he said, rising from his chair and standing in front of me to make sure he had my complete attention. He stared me down until I raised my head and looked him in the eyes. He reached for my hands and squeezed them hard. I was already wincing when he said, "I want you to help us raise the child."

I felt the final piece of myself break away from our marriage. We had decided long ago not to have children of our own. Between his courtroom and my classroom, we didn't need any more humans to take care of, little or big. But at his words, I felt a rise of bitter jealousy that he would now have a child of his own and I would not, ever.

Without saying a word, for I could think of none to say, I turned and went into our bedroom, closing the door and pulling back the blankets of our bed so I could curl up beneath them. Every fiber of my body felt frozen, shocked into stillness by the latest revelation of my husband's betrayal. I lay there for hours, trying to imagine what to do next. I needed some time to determine what to do with the remainder of my life, which was starting to feel like an old purse, its contents strewn all over the floor.

As always, when I was sad or afraid, I longed to speak to my mother. She had died just after I graduated from college I had been so busy with my very first class, I hadn't properly grieved. My sadness was buried beneath piles of paper that comprised my life, from the reams of my master's thesis to the thick folders that contained my daily lesson plans. Distracted by the details of a busy life, I tried not to dwell on her absence. But in my darkest moments, I was tossed back in time like a rag doll, and the empty space in my heart felt raw and painful, like a part of me had been ripped away.

I missed the days when I was her child, safe and adored. I wanted to return to the summers of my youth, when my biggest challenge was lying on the grass and finding images in puffs of clouds as they passed over the lake.

The idea seeped into my awareness, spreading into the darkest corners of my mind like bright colors rinsed from a painter's palette, and the decision came to me fully formed, before I was even aware I was considering it. It was the only thing I could do. I had to go home.

3

The next day, I packed some things into the back of my silver Prius and drove two hours to Lily Dale, the little lakeside community in Western New York where I was raised. It was a place where people talk to the dead.

I wanted to see Maeve O'Toole, my mother's best friend. She was the only person left in my life who had loved me since I was born. Although I had been appallingly bad at responding to her faithful stream of cards and emails, her communications always made me feel as if I were still connected to the people and places of my childhood. And though she knew I'd never had much interest in the spiritualist religion that inspired the birth of Lily Dale more than a hundred and thirty years ago, she made it clear the little town would always be my home.

"Darling girl," Maeve said when she saw me through her screen door, standing forlornly on her porch. I tried to smile at her words because I have always felt like Maeve's darling girl, but silent tears spilled from my eyes. We embraced, and I inhaled the familiar scent of the incense she burned before doing a reading. Her white hair was wrapped in a bun at the nape of her neck, her bangs trimmed neatly over sharp blue eyes, which surveyed me thoughtfully when we pulled out of our hug. "What's happened to you?"

"I need to talk to my mom," I said, wiping away my tears.

Maeve looked into my eyes for a moment and then nodded. "Yes, you do. But not right now. You look tired, my girl. You need to rest."

She pulled me into her comfortable living room, which was unchanged since I had last seen it years before. I sat down across from her and told her of the challenges I'd been facing: my worry that the cancer had returned and my husband's betrayal. Bless her heart; she didn't look the least bit horrified, perhaps because she'd heard so many sad stories in her work as a medium, where she communicated with the spirit world for grieving humans who longed to speak to their dead. She reached for my hand and held it tight.

"Why don't you stay here with me for a few weeks, and we'll figure the rest out later, " she said in a tone that made me feel ten years old again, transporting me back to the days when she and my mother were raising their children together. Maeve's own two daughters were my dearest friends from childhood, but I'd kept in little better contact with them than I had with her. And yet, being back in Lily Dale, it felt like nothing had changed.

Maeve put me up in the small guest apartment over her garage. From the tiny porch, I could see the entire community with its walkways, courtyards, and cottages surrounded by thick woods of ancient trees. I felt comforted by the immersion into my childhood memories. For the first time in a long while, I was able to breathe.

I spent the following days cocooned by the gentle energy of the place. While my neighbors communed with the dead, I poked and prodded the deaths in my own life, grieving not just the destruction of my marriage and the loss of my vitality and wellness, but also finally turning my attention to the deaths of my mother and grandmother. I could feel their presence in this place they both loved. My grandmother was a tiny woman with dark hair and piercing eyes. She was one of the most beloved mediums ever to reside at Lily Dale, and many said I resembled her. Then there was my mother who, with her slender frame and long legs, would amble through the community in her cropped pants and baby doll flats looking more like a displaced starlet than a psychic medium.

My grandmother often told me that my mother was even better at talking to the dead than she was. The information my mom obtained from spirit was so much more precise than my grandmother's, and my mother had a large and loyal following among those who returned to the community each summer. But she didn't love the work like my grandmother did. The sadness and neediness of her clients seemed to seep into her soul and steal away her graceful good humor. And then the cancer came, invading her body with a vengeance, just as it was likely doing to me now. Shortly after I left Lily Dale for college, my mom crossed over. My grandmother, brokenhearted and unafraid of death, passed shortly after. I was left without any family until I married Michael. And now he was gone, too.

So, I grieved, quietly at first and then angrily. I would walk the little beach late at night after most of the tourists had left, flinging rocks into the lake and swearing softly to myself. I cursed my husband for abandoning me and was angry with my mother and grandmother as well, for leaving me far too soon. With nothing to occupy my time but reflection, and with the recurrence of the cancer looming over me like a swinging sword, I felt hopeless, as if my life were already over.

I wondered how I could be fifty-four years old, yet so uncertain. What had happened to the part of me that always knew exactly what to do? I went over those questions in my mind but found no answers. My hopelessness grew. What was I going to do with the rest of my life, I asked myself over and over. I had a sonogram scheduled at the end of the month. What if the cancer had returned? If I were dying, should I go back to Michael? Maybe I could find a way to live with his infidelity. What about my job? Should I warn my principal I might not be returning? After endless rounds of questions with no answers, I grew frustrated by my own speculations and sadness. Maeve was busy tending the flocks of visitors who came to Lily Dale during the summer months. Her promise to help me connect with my mother seemed forgotten, but I understood. As a leader of the community, she didn't have much time between private readings and organizing the daily events, which included the services each morning at the assembly hall and the afternoon gatherings at "Inspiration Stump" in the woods.

Out of sheer desperation and with nothing more interesting to fill my days, I decided to enroll in one of the many classes offered at Lily Dale during the season for those who wanted to learn more about such topics as mediumship, energy healing, or past-life regression.

Maeve was starting her annual "Introduction to Mediumship" course, and I began attending the twice-a-week classes. It wasn't that I felt a need to talk to random dead people. I felt a need to talk to *my* dead people. Contrary to every logical, hard-won belief I'd ever held, I'd crumbled when facing the worst emotional disaster of my life. I'd turned my attention to the afterlife in the desperate hope that somebody was there.

I shouldn't have been surprised to find myself back at Lily Dale looking for answers, but I was. Growing up, my mother and grandmother's mediumship abilities paid the bills and allowed us to live in the little community. I had never considered mediumship to be a skill I would practice. Like many adult children who turn away from the religion in which they were raised, I'd had no emotional connection to spiritualism. I simply did not believe. Skepticism was my birthright, inherent in my genes. My conception had been the result of a brief relationship between my mother and a scientist who'd come looking to communicate with the spirits of dead inventors. She'd always told me I got my thirst for learning from him.

Apparently, my father had won her over with his good looks and magnificent brain, but he was a humorless man with wide, unblinking eyes, and he'd had no interest in raising a child. That was fine, because after he'd signed away all rights to me, I never had much interest in him, either.

My childhood was filled with the love of my mother and grandmother and all the strange and wonderful neighbors who lived with us in Lily Dale. But my father's skepticism flowed through my veins like a liquid legacy. I had no use for the secrets of the afterlife that my mother and grandmother spent their lives exploring. Living required all my energy. I didn't much care what came after. And I certainly didn't care much for the God of my childhood. A person can't work in a gritty, urban neighborhood and believe in a fair and loving deity. If there was a God, he was surely not doing the job that we all gave him so much credit for. If there was a God, he was a partial God, and I didn't have any desire to know him.

Yet, especially in this place, I missed my mom, and the need to connect with her, just one more time, filled me with a consuming desire. I was like the little match girl in the children's fable, a freezing, orphaned child lighting matches in the icy darkness, hoping for the warmth that a glimpse of her could provide. I was suddenly quite willing in my frozen despair, to consider it possible to find her in spirit and talk with her once more.

4

After many dreamless nights, my mother finally came to me. It wasn't nearly enough. When I awoke, she disappeared into a misty memory, and I'd felt a wrenching sadness as if I'd lost her again. In the dream, I was alone on the streets of Lily Dale and I saw her walking toward me, the rising sun creating a violet aura around her. I couldn't believe it was her, until she got close enough to look me in the eye. She was vibrant and beautiful. I was overjoyed.

"Mama," I'd shouted like a child, running into her arms. Tears flowed from my eyes and she grabbed me and held me tight, whispering into my ear.

"Sweetheart," she'd crooned, with the silky voice I'd always found so comforting. "Don't be afraid." They were the same words she would whisper when I was a child and she'd come in my room late at night to calm me from bad dreams.

She'd pulled away, tipped my chin, and held it so I had nowhere to look but into her eyes. They were deep pools of light, and I stared into them, entranced by their beauty. "He's with you now. Everything is going to be just fine."

It lasted only seconds, and then my mother was gone. When I awoke, I was reluctant to open my eyes, still feeling her strong arms around me and smelling the clean scent of her dark hair. I dragged myself from beneath the covers, unwilling to wake fully, and walked sleepily to the stove to turn on a flame under the teakettle. I leaned against the counter, eyes closed, trying to recall the dream. What had she said? He's with me? *Who's* with me? God? The only other "he" I could think of was my father, and I didn't want to see either one of them. I wanted my mom. The longing to be with her was palpable. In those few seconds, looking into her eyes, I saw myself as she saw me, not as an aging woman whose life had crashed into pieces, but as her beloved child. Within her gaze, I knew my life was not such a mess at all, but just a moment of darkness blocking the light. Still, when I woke, I couldn't imagine how to rebuild myself into the woman I saw in my mother's eyes, no matter who was here to help me.

The kettle boiled and I made myself a cup of lemon pepper tea, using a tea bag from a box in the cupboard. I carried the cup out to the small balcony of the apartment and lowered myself into the old, pink wicker chair that was the only piece of furniture there.

My doctor's appointment, to determine if the cancer had returned, was several weeks away. Until then, I had nothing but time.

I heard a buzz from my cell phone in the kitchen. I sighed. Michael was calling again. Since my arrival in Lily Dale, I'd never answered his daily phone calls and deleted his messages without listening to them. I had already heard everything he had to say. I debated whether I should shut my phone off completely for a while, but decided I liked knowing that Michael thought of me each day, and that he was clearly sorry to have hurt me. I also felt a surprising sense of freedom being unattached from my husband. While I knew I would always feel love for him, our connection had lost its electricity long ago. In my ruminations since our break-up, I had unearthed an awareness that the same vague loneliness, which had pushed him away, had been plaguing me as well. I had just never really given it my full attention until now.

A voice called up from the sidewalk beneath the porch, breaking the silence of the morning. I recognized Maeve's brisk tones. "Hello! Rebecca?"

I stood, pulling my fluffy, yellow bathrobe tighter, and leaned over the balcony. "Good morning, Maeve," I called back, waving my teacup in greeting. "How are you?"

She was dressed for the day in a white blouse and black pants, pearls draped around her neck, her white hair in an up-do. She stared up at me for a moment as if considering what to say. "I...talked to your mother this morning," she said.

I could feel my heart beating faster. "Really?"

She smiled tentatively. "I was making the bed, and she showed up for a little chat."

Maeve spoke as if my mom had just walked over from our house down the street. I did a quick inventory of all the people I knew who might consider Maeve's words to be crazy, but was painfully aware of how much I wanted to believe my dead mother had just shown up in her best friend's bedroom.

"I dreamt of her," I admitted. "But, she disappeared after just a few words."

Maeve tipped her head, putting her hand over her eyes like a visor to shield them from the glare of the sun. "Maybe it was easier for her to come to me," she replied, eyes locked for a few seconds on mine before she looked down to check the watch on her wrist. "I'd like to tell you more, but I've got an early reading. Why don't you meet me after you get dressed, and we'll walk to the assembly hall together?"

"I'd like that," I replied, giving Maeve a wave and sitting back down in the rocker, feeling like a kid who's been away at summer camp for far too many weeks, whose mom is finally calling on the phone. I couldn't wait to talk to her again. I took one last sip of my cold tea and stared out into the little community, with its colorful cottages nestled in the protection of ancient trees. A smattering of visitors had begun to make their way through the front gates of Lily Dale, many hoping to talk to their dead, like me.

I knew that Maeve was trying to break through my skepticism and unearth my sense of wonder. But for the past few weeks, the only real emotion I could muster was doubt. Doubt in my abilities to have a full life, doubt in my abilities to love another human well enough so that they would never leave me, and doubt that I even wanted to live another day.

In that first mediumship class two weeks ago, it had been especially hard to stay focused. I tried taking notes, but it wasn't long before I was absentmindedly doodling on my notepad. There were three of us in Maeve's "Introduction to Mediumship," and she spent much of the first hour explaining the basic philosophies of the Spiritualist Church, where members believe that mediumship, prophecy and healing are expressions of God. It felt just like the religious instruction classes my mom sent me to when I was a child at the Spiritualist church down the street. I let Maeve's words wash over me and took some comfort in their familiarity. Maeve explained how spiritualists believe that mediumship can be taught, and my curiosity was finally aroused when she reminded us that the human imagination is where all such learning is inspired. As a teacher, I knew that. If you can make a child's eyes widen with delight or curiosity, you can teach them pretty much anything. I tried to do that every day in my classroom. We would count giant bubbles that I made with a wand dipped in soap to teach the basics of math and subtraction. "Here comes one bubble. Add that one. Two now. Oops, that bubble burst, let's subtract it from our total." The kids loved the bubbles. So did I.

I taught geography by releasing newly hatched butterflies out the windows of my classroom, and I would encourage my students to wonder where those butterflies might go. So I was inspired by the possibility of using my imagination to connect to my mother. From within the safe circle of Maeve's classes and the cocoon of my garage apartment, I began to feel the healing of my heart and the tickle of the possibility that life might hold more than I believed.

I stood and stretched, reaching my arms overhead and then bent to gather my teacup. It was time to ready myself for the morning assembly.

Each day for the past week, as part of my classwork, but also because I had nothing else to do, I had sat near some of the other mediums in the giant assembly hall as they connected with spirit for visitors who attended the morning reading service. I enjoyed watching the faces of those who were told their dead loved ones were present, but I felt a bit sad for all the others whose people in spirit did not show.

I dressed as quickly as I could, reaching for my favorite summer dress, a sleeveless pink sheath, and stepping into a pair of sandals. I stood in front of the bathroom mirror and surveyed my short hair, which had grown in surprisingly well since the chemo. I grabbed a container of hair gel and applied a dab, moving my curls around into little tufts, happy to see that my new, natural dark color was far more pepper than salt. I leaned over the sink and stared at my face and the Mediterranean skin I inherited from my mother. Despite the physical battering I'd taken from the chemotherapy and the emotional assault of my husband's betrayal, I appreciated the way my face and my body had survived. The furies may have been at war within me, but I didn't look as if I were one of the walking wounded.

A few minutes later, I let myself into Maeve's cottage with the key she'd given me and surveyed the serene living room. I loved the little house with its views of the water through paned-glass windows. Maeve's home was built in the late 1800s, and the decor was of the era, with stained glass lamps and upholstered armchairs. I could hear the murmurs coming from the reading room and I was reminded of my childhood, when I would come home and find my mother or grandmother similarly engaged.

Sitting among the neatly arranged pillows on Maeve's couch, I thought of my father. After many unsuccessful years in his laboratory, he became obsessed with the idea of trying to contact the spirit of Nikola Tesla, a brilliant Serbian scientist whose electrical inventions helped light half a nation. My father determined he would need a medium to help him, but once he laid eyes on my mother, his dream of a scientific breakthrough was tossed aside like a lab coat as he began his ardent pursuit of her. Unfortunately, when she read for him, the spirit of Tesla did not show. That was the way things worked with mediumship. She always said it was impossible to predict who would appear from the world of spirit. Instead, my father's dead mother came through for the reading, holding his favorite childhood pet, a one-eyed Tabby cat named Sanders. After describing the old woman and cat in precise detail, my mother delivered a loving message. His mother wanted him to know there was more to life than what he could find in a laboratory, and that if he spent a little more time in the pursuit of simple joys and human relationships, his mind would open to all the creative possibilities of his work.

That wasn't what my father wanted to hear. He wanted the secrets Tesla had taken to his grave. Instead, he got a maternal lecture. My father felt he had been tricked. Though he was obsessed with my mother, he could never reconcile his inability to substantiate her gifts. During their brief affair, she came to feel like a butterfly pinned to parchment as he questioned her over and over on how she deduced the correct descriptions of his mother and cat. Where did the information come from, he demanded to know. She tried to explain that the images had simply appeared in her mind's eye, but he was never satisfied with that answer and imagined she had somehow gotten the details from someone who knew him or a photograph he hadn't known existed. His insistence on my mother's trickery was far sillier than the idea of her talking to the dead, and his obsession with provable facts was his undoing, at least in his relationship with my mom. It ended as quickly as it began, despite the sage advice of his ghostly mother. His loss was the lifetime he could have spent in the warmth of my mother's love. My loss, I could see from the vantage point of time, was that I apparently was to never have a relationship with a man who would stay. And yet, my father's obsession with proof was something I clearly understood as I sat in Maeve's living room, waiting for her to help me talk to my dead mother.

I heard a rustling from the reading room and knew the session was ending. A few moments later, Maeve came out with a middle-aged, heavyset woman. The woman wiped away a tear and hugged Maeve tightly. "I cannot thank you enough. I haven't been able to sleep for the past year since he died. Now that I know he's okay, I feel that I can begin to heal."

As the woman left, I watched Maeve's eyes follow her and I was touched by the serenity and affection I saw there. "You love this work," I said.

She nodded. "I cannot think of anything I'd rather do. That woman came to me with a broken heart, and I was able to connect with her dead son and help her begin to mend it. He told her he'd left a note for her in the pages of a bible in his bedroom. I'm hoping that she'll remember to call me if she finds it." Then she laughed, putting her hand up to her forehead to push a stray white curl back into place. "You'd think I'd be past the point where I needed validation, but I never get tired of the little miracles that spirit sends our way. It's what keeps me going."

Maeve headed back into her reading room to blow out the candles and shut off the lights. She called to me over her shoulder as she moved about the room. "So, speaking of validation, your mom wants you to know how happy she is that you're home."

My heart began beating a little faster. "Oh, yeah?" I tried to sound casual, but I was hoping for much more than a welcome home. "Where is she?"

"I'll tell you on the way," Maeve said, holding the door.

We headed down the path past the lake to the assembly hall. "So," I asked again. "Where has she been?"

"I'm not quite sure. But she looked lovely and happy. I'd forgotten how beautiful she was." Maeve sighed.

I stopped dead in the middle of the sidewalk. She was *not* going to give me some vague details and think I'd be satisfied. I wanted my own note in the bedroom, like the lady she'd just read for. "I need more than that, Maeve," I insisted, feeling like a stubborn child, refusing to move until I got more from her.

"Well, she did ask me to do this," Maeve said. She reached for me and pulled me close. I resisted at first, but Maeve was strong. She held me tight. "Your mom sent you this," she said softly. "Just breathe for a second, and feel her energy."

I tried to comply, but I was unsettled by our location on the sidewalk and my fear that someone would see us standing there, hugging. Then I felt a shift in Maeve's energy and suddenly it seemed that somehow, my mother was holding me. "Everything is going to be fine," Maeve told me, repeating my mother's words from the dream. "He's coming."

I pulled away and asked her, my voice rising like an angry five-year-old's, "Maeve, who is coming?"

Maeve opened her eyes. "Why, my dear," she said, shaking her head and looking as surprised as I was by what just occurred, "I have absolutely no idea."

5

The visitors filed down the rows of the old assembly hall and as I waited for the service to begin, I was still thinking about what had just occurred in the street. Dreaming about my mother's embrace was one thing, but feeling as if my dead mom had somehow entered Maeve's body to give me a hug gave me pause. Suddenly my life was awash with the unexpected, and I was doing things I never dreamed I'd do, like sitting in the assembly hall and taking part in the morning mediumship service. I would never have imagined that I would ever give a reading to anyone. But in Maeve's class, I was discovering that I was fairly good at receiving what appeared to be afterlife information and that I enjoyed doing it.

I thought back to a recent class when I gave my very first reading. I'd been sitting across from my classmate, Tracy, and we'd just said a brief prayer of protection as Maeve had taught us to do, when I saw a little dog in my imagination. It was a fluffy ball of yellow fur, and I watched it jump happily as a little girl approached. The girl had big, blue eyes, and red curls. I saw her scoop up the dog and carry it over to a wobbly pink bicycle where she placed it in the basket attached to the handlebars. She climbed on the bike and went wheeling down the road with the puppy's head bobbing from the basket. It was like watching a reel of those old movies my mom used to shoot on her Kodak camera. Stunned by the appearance of such clear and unexpected images, I opened my eyes and looked at Tracy, who was waiting for me to say something. I told her what I'd seen in my imagination.

She smiled, her eyes wide. "That's Gwendolyn," she said. "The best dog ever."

I was so shocked at this new ability, my brain shut down in startled self-defense. I saw nothing more that day. But after a couple of sessions, I began to get comfortable. As Maeve encouraged us to relax and not try too hard, I started getting reels of information, with visits from other spirits related to my classmates, including Tracy's mom, and Maeve's sister.

In the beginning, the visions didn't speak. When I saw Tracy's mom, she was baking in the kitchen. I watched as she clapped her hands and was immediately surrounded by a little cloud of flour dust. It was funny. I smiled. "Your mom liked to bake," I said to Tracy and was pleased when she nodded in response.

There was even a visit from the dead wife of my other classmate, Albert. But when I saw her in my head, she didn't move at all. She just stood there, looking out at me with compassionate blue eyes. She was slender, with blonde hair that curled into soft waves at her shoulders, and she wore dark red lipstick. Albert was so happy when I described her. He had only been widowed for a few years, and it was clear that the pain of losing her was fresh. It felt nice to bring a smile to his face.

I was amazed at how easy it was, but I still wasn't confident. I had already guessed wrong a few times, misinterpreting the information that popped into my head. During the last class, I was reading for one of the volunteers that Maeve had invited. Her name was Joy, and she was a cheerful, middle-aged brunette who had been recruited so we could practice our skills on someone we had never met. I had just closed my eyes when I saw a soldier sitting next to his gun in a muddy trench. I watched him light a cigarette with shaking hands, and I was touched by his fear and homesickness, emotions that I felt briefly in my body as if they were my own. It was dark in the trench and I couldn't see him very well, so I just presumed, given Joy's age, that it was her father. "I see your dad," I told her over-confidently. "He's in a trench in a war zone, and he's scared. I saw him lighting a cigarette."

Joy shook her head, puzzled. "No. My dad was never in the service."

I was surprised, but decided just to ask the soldier for more information, as Maeve recommended. In my imagination, I silently asked him to show me more, and he reached into his shirt and pulled out a photo of the woman across from me and stared at the photo lovingly.

"He's looking at a photo of you," I said.

She thought for a while, then nearly shouted in surprise. "Oh, my God, that's Timmy. We had a giant crush on each other when we were teenagers, but I lost track of him after we moved. I'd heard he was drafted and sent to Vietnam." She sat back in her chair and breathed a long sigh. "I'd always wondered if he had survived the war."

I smiled. I felt like a little kid finally learning to ride a bike. Maeve had told us that it was easy to talk to the dead. Anyone could do it, she said. And if I was doing it, that was surely true.

Joy watched me intently. "Do you see anything else about him?"

I closed my eyes once more and waited for images to appear. There he was again, standing patiently, as if waiting for me to ask him more questions. He was tall and skinny, and wore ripped and dirty battle fatigues. I asked the young soldier if he had survived the war. Through a quick change of scenes and some charade-like movements, I saw that Timmy did not die in Vietnam. In an instant, he was dressed in jeans and a red-and black-checked flannel shirt. He looked sad and tired. I felt my heart clench. It didn't feel like his life went well after he came home from the war. Timmy showed me an image of himself dumping pills into a glass of what looked like whiskey. In an enthusiastic re-creation, he demonstrated how he died, in what he seemed to want me to understand was an accidental overdose. He clasped his hands to his heart and fell upon his bed. Then he opened one eye and winked playfully at me, before I saw his spirit rising from the remains of the human form that lay in his disheveled bed. He smiled delightedly as he rose upward, again pulling the photo of Joy out of his shirt and giving it a hug.

I interpreted as best I could, telling her about his death and what was clearly an overdose. "He's very funny, showing me how he died," I said. "He wants you to know he's very happy where he is, and he is sending you love."

Remembering the little vignette, I sat in my chair at the assembly and shook my head. I didn't know if I was actually communicating with the dead, or if I had just imagined Timmy and the messages he sought to convey. But hearing from a long lost boyfriend made Joy very happy. And that made me happy. Learning these skills and conjuring up people's loved ones in my head, was like taking a sip from the elixir of eternity, and it made me wonder what else I had been wrong about.

6

As I sat near the stage with several of the mediums who would be reading that morning, I thought of how this giant, old hall was one of the places where I felt most connected to my mother and grandmother. They had spent many mornings of my childhood upon its wooden stage, and sometimes I would leave my friends and slip inside the hall, standing by the big doors in the back of the room to watch them work. The scenes I remembered best were similar to the one before me. I watched as the hundred or so visitors settled into the rows, the old wooden seats creaking in response to their movements. I thought about how, throughout my life, I was often asked how my mom and grandmother were able to do what they did.

It was challenging to explain. My mom said that some mediums heard words in their head. Some saw pictures in their mind's eye. During readings at the assemblies, the dead would appear in my mother's imagination, sometimes standing patiently in a line, waiting for her attention. With her eyes open, she would scan the room and find she was drawn to a certain area. As she rested her eyes on a dozen or so anxious folks assembled in a section, a specific person would snag her gaze. She would consult the lineup in her head, and usually someone would step forward and give her an indication of who they were, maybe holding a milk crate if they were a dairy farmer, or wearing a nurse's uniform. Then she would ask, "I see a nurse. Do you know of a nurse that has passed?" Inevitably, that person did.

My grandmother, on the other hand, saw energy. She told me she would see the light shift around the person she was supposed to read, and when she focused her gaze on that person, information would appear in her head. She would see a letter or symbol, and when the person confirmed that the image held significance to them, the information would start to flow into her mind, as if a faucet had been turned on. Sometimes a spirit would mime the information, as they did for me when I started. Other times, she would hear language, such as words from a deceased mom or dad saying, "Tell her not to marry that guy." Why the details came in that way, no one could ever explain to me. I didn't understand why dead people didn't come right out and say, "Hey, I'm her Aunt Sophie from Albuquerque." Perhaps it involved a certain skill level from those in the afterlife. Or from those in this life. But either way, sharing the information required a great deal of confidence from the medium to whom it was delivered.

My grandmother told me it was important to believe that the dead were returning for divine reasons, so loved ones left behind could have hope and not grieve too much or too long. It wasn't until I began taking classes that I really understood. I relaxed into my own intuition and tapped the ability Maeve said each human had to connect with those from the beyond. I learned in my classes that my senses, like my grandmother's, allowed me to see the movement of energy around a person. If I observed them with a soft gaze while in a relaxed state, I could sometimes see gently undulating waves of energy, like looking at the energy around a patio grill when it's fired up and ready to use on a hot day. It was barely perceptible, but enough to draw my attention to the person I needed to connect with. It had already happened a couple of times for me, when I'd been sitting near the stage with the more experienced mediums, but I hadn't yet had the nerve to stand up and give a reading.

I likely wouldn't have done so that day, had I not seen the shape of a man suddenly appear at the side of the room. It was the first time I saw him fully formed. He was standing behind a woman of about twenty, her blonde hair pulled back into a ponytail. I could see right through his image and couldn't make out any specific details, but he was clearly a spirit. As I stared at him, he seemed to play with me. He was there, then he was not, and I wasn't sure whether I was imagining him. But then he would appear again, and move slightly behind the girl like an undulating halo. Suddenly, as if remembering a forgotten dream, the final moments of my last day of school flooded back into my memory. I remembered the sparks of light that had appeared in my classroom and brought such delight to Charlie. The same sparks had appeared when I was ending my marriage with Michael. I had completely forgotten those moments because at the time, my life was crashing into a thousand pieces. But sitting on that stage, I recognized the energy that seemed to beckon for my attention. And I couldn't help but smile.

Maeve stood and walked over to the podium, calling the session to order. "Good morning," she said cheerily to the group that was suddenly still. "Welcome to the Lily Dale Assembly." She opened a prayer book that was on the podium. "We welcome all religions here, because in the Spiritualist Church, we believe that we all come from the same source. The only thing that makes us different from other religions is that we believe it is possible to communicate with those who have crossed over into spirit, and many of us strive to learn to do so. In a reading service like this one, you will see how it's done, although we never know who is going to come through, or what they will say."

A toddler sitting on his father's lap in the front row cooed and waved his arms. Maeve smiled at him. "We welcome everyone to our community and our church. We're not quite as formal as other churches you may have experienced. But we know we are doing the work of the Lord." She looked down at the book and opened it to a ribboned page. "So now, we will start with a prayer and ask God to bless these events." She recited reverent words that were familiar and dear to those in the community, and then the reading service began.

I watched as the first medium, Henry O'Connor, stood and assessed the assembly. Henry had worked with me and the other two students in my class during the past weeks of mediumship training. A slender, elderly man with neatly trimmed gray beard and mustache, he was confident and impressively accurate.

"May I come to you, Miss?" he asked of a woman sitting about ten rows back to his right. Several people looked around to see if he was pointing at them. "Yes, you, in the pink shirt." He smiled warmly. The woman nodded, and Henry began. He closed his eyes and spoke in a serious tenor voice. "I have a man here. He's wearing an old-fashioned cowboy hat." Her eyes widened and she nodded. "He says that he is with you every day. He appreciates that you put the flowers on his grave, but it makes him sad that you are still grieving for him after all these years…"

I was watching Henry when I saw the spirit again, off to the side of the hall. I looked around to see if anyone else could see him, but everyone was watching Henry. Mine were the only eyes turned towards the wall. The hazy figure thickened, and I was able to make out his legs, arms, and head. It appeared he was looking right at me, and I decided to try and communicate with him, as Maeve had taught us. Silently, I sent him a question in my mind. "Who are you?"

The spirit pointed to a girl with a blonde ponytail seated near him. I was taken back by the awareness that he wanted me to do a reading during the morning assembly.

"I can't do that," I replied to him, the unspoken words sounding loud in my head.

The spirit seemed able to understand. He nodded his head up and down slowly and pointed at the girl again. "Yes, you can," he seemed to be saying.

Uncertain, but unable to say no to the persistent spirit, I nudged Maeve and leaned over to her. "Can I read this morning?"

Her brows rose. "Are you ready?"

I shrugged and whispered, "I'm seeing a spirit, and he's not taking no for an answer."

Maeve smiled. "Then you are ready. Of course you can read."

My teacher turned to the medium waiting to read next, a white-haired woman in a long skirt and flowered blouse named Genevieve, who was sitting beside her. "Rebecca wants to do a reading when you're finished, okay?"

Genevieve looked at me, her eyes crinkled in a smile. "That would be lovely."

Of course, their complete confidence in me turned up the heat. My nerves kicked in. I began to perspire. What if the image disappeared completely?

What if I tried to communicate and ended up with nothing to say to the ponytailed girl? I sat there for about ten minutes as Genevieve did a reading for a young man in jeans and a T-shirt. I remembered how my mother and grandmother had dreamed of my doing exactly this, working as a medium in Lily Dale. I never imagined I would consider such a thing. I had wanted a normal life, like so many of my friends at school whose family members didn't talk to the dead. It wasn't until I was older that I came to understand being just like everyone else involved giving away parts of yourself that were unique and dear.

And now, thanks to my recently expanded open-mindedness, motivated by being far too close to the precipice of existence, I was at the assembly waiting to communicate with the spirit of a dead man who appeared to be on a mission. Given the course of my life, believing I could do this was the same level of crazy as believing I could fly. But I had come too far to turn back. The precipice was waiting. I would have to trust that I had wings.

Finally, it was my turn to read. I took a deep breath. Then I walked out into the aisle, closer to the crowd, near where I had first seen the shimmering image and pointed to the ponytailed girl. "May I come to you?" I asked.

The girl nodded, her eyes wide with curiosity. "Yes, please."

I stared into her hopeful eyes and relaxed my gaze. By diverting my attention to the pensive face of my subject, I was relieved to see the image had returned, and I could just make it out behind her. Here goes nothing, I thought.

"I see a man with you," I said with as much fake confidence as I could muster. The girl nodded, and her face lit up with a smile. The energy seemed to bounce behind her, perhaps to affirm my words. His movement reminded me of the kind of hopping about that I did as a child with a jump rope. He was apparently giving me a clue. "He's very energetic," I said, smiling a little at the obvious statement. "He appears to be jumping rope."

The girl laughed. "It's my grandfather. We used to jump rope together when I was little."

The image stopped, and the energy appeared to cross his arms over his chest as if he was holding something. In my head, I heard a man's voice say distinctly, "Tell her I have Ferdinand."

What? I cleared my throat. He nodded again, a swift and decisive affirmation.

"He said to tell you he has Ferdinand."

The girl let out a delighted giggle. "No way."

I shrugged, encouraged by my success but trying not to get overconfident. "Way," I responded.

"Ferdinand was my little beagle," she explained. "My grandfather would try to jump rope with me, and the beagle would watch us and charge at my sneaker laces. That's so funny. I'd forgotten all about that."

I closed my eyes again and finally saw him, an older man, slender and fit, with wild white hair askew from his efforts, trying to slowly swing the light rope so that he and a little girl could jump together. It was a silly sight, made sillier by the little dog I saw leap towards the girl's shoes and get tangled in the rope. Even though I saw the grandfather as an old man, I didn't get the sense that his energy was that of someone old. I continued with the reading, quieting my mind to see if there was more information forthcoming.

I heard him again, in my head. His voice was deep and clear, and I felt it reverberate through my body. "Tell her I am always with her. I was there with her today when she was at the mailbox, looking for the letter. Tell her not to worry. It will come."

It was pretty amazing. I could hear *and* see him. I delivered the next message. "He says he was there with you at the mailbox today, and that you should not worry. The letter is coming."

The girl was visibly relieved. "I just graduated from a two-year college. I'm applying for my bachelor's degree. Does he know which school?"

In my head, the old man crouched in the pose of a wrestler about to take on an opponent. Then I saw the opponent. It was a giant grizzly bear. The old man winked conspiratorially at me, and I laughed aloud, understanding immediately. "Did you apply to a school with a grizzly bear as a mascot?" I asked.

"Yes, I did! " Her eyes lit with delight. "Did I get accepted?"

"According to your grandfather," I replied. The energy behind the girl, still barely detectable as a human shape, leaned over her and kissed the top of her head. He then turned his attention to the woman beside her and did the same.

I got his message loud and clear. "He says that he wants you to know he is always there for you, and he just kissed the top of your head. He did the same to you," I added, addressing the woman who sat beside the ponytailed girl.

She was an elegant beauty wearing a colorful headscarf and hoop earrings. Both had tears in their eyes as they hugged. The light behind the girl brightened, and it appeared that the spirit was about to say something more, but I heard Maeve's voice behind me calling the assembly to a close. The reading was over. The image disappeared as if someone had hit a switch.

"Thank you all for coming this morning. We hope you enjoy the rest of the day. Don't forget, there's an afternoon service at Inspirational Stump in the woods. Where ever you are heading, our wish is that you carry

God's blessings with you and share them with all you meet."

The room filled with noise as people rose from their seats and collected their things. The woman who'd been seated next to the girl I'd just read made her way down the aisle to where I was standing, still amazed by what had just occurred.

She reached for my hand. "I just want to thank you," she said. "My daughter has been especially missing her grandfather lately. They were very close."

I took her hand in mine and clasped it with my other. "You have no idea how honored I am to have been able to give her that information."

The woman squinted at me through dark blue eyes. "My father and I had a difficult relationship. I was never able to quite forgive him for abandoning my mom and me when I was young. He left one day and didn't come back for ten years. He expected me to be delighted when he returned. I wasn't."

I nodded in sympathy. I surely could understand what it felt like to have a man betray you and break your heart.

"At the end of his life, he had nowhere else to go, so I invited him to stay with us," she continued. "I never really got over being mad at him, but my daughter couldn't resist his charming and silly ways. She adored him."

The woman smiled, as if in relief. "You know, I really needed him to show up today for her. I'm kind of happy that he finally came through for me. For her. I just wanted to thank you." I watched her walk away and catch up to her daughter who was standing just outside the giant double doors. They embraced and I exhaled a long breath.

Finally, I was the last one left in the hall. I sat down in one of the wooden chairs and took the moment to enjoy what had just occurred. While I had had a variety of hits and misses in class, this was the first time I had actually helped someone with my skills. It hadn't been a long message, but it was clearly information the girl needed to hear.

Beyond that, it felt to me like the moment when a student finally understands a math problem or a sentence in a poem, providing both the teacher and the student with a small piece of time lit by grace. I felt like I'd received a blessing too.

7

Dusk was settling later that day, as I walked from dinner at the little cafe near the assembly hall to my class, treading carefully down the dirt path to Maeve's bungalow on the lake's edge. Like many cottage communities, Lily Dale remained alive on summer evenings, with residents enjoying gentle lake breezes from decks and porches, as others in small groups passed by on the sidewalks, often in animated conversations.

I walked up to Maeve's door and knocked twice on the wood of the screen. It was unlocked, but I waited for her to call out, "It's open. Come in!" There was soft music playing as I entered the living room where Maeve waited in a wingback chair. I could smell the scent of patchouli from her candles. "Hello, love," she said, waving me into the room. "Come in, and make yourself comfortable. The others are on their way." I leaned down to give her a hug, and went to sit in a nearby chair.

"You did well at the assembly this morning, " Maeve said, smiling.

I nodded. "I wanted to talk to you about that. This guy has been kind of showing up..." Before I could finish my sentence, we were distracted by the arrival of my fellow students.

Albert walked in first, ducking his head to fit his tall frame through the door. He looked down at us, as if from a great distance, and half-smiled. Albert was a retired college professor, slender and slightly balding, a deeply serious fellow who didn't say much in our little class, but who listened intently to every word. He wore aviator spectacles and was simply dressed in an untucked grey cotton shirt and khaki pants. I didn't know much about him, except that he lost his wife from the terrible injuries she sustained after a car accident involving a drunk driver. He told us he had been missing her intently and was taking the class to see if he could somehow connect with her spirit. I was never sure whether it was shyness or grief that he carried into the room with him each time he entered, but he always made me feel a little sad when I saw him.

In contrast, Tracy bounded into the room right behind him, dropping herself so enthusiastically onto the over-stuffed couch where he sat that he bounced a bit on his own cushion. If someone were studying human energy, my two classmates would be perfect subjects upon which to practice. Tracy was a slight young woman with brown hair she wore straight to her shoulders that always looked windblown and in need of a comb. She dressed in long skirts and cropped T-shirts, like a teenager from my era when kids listened to protest songs and practiced free love. She had big brown eyes that, when directed upon you, seemed filled with acceptance and understanding. She was only twenty-nine, but already a pretty good medium, though there was never a sense of competition in our classes. We were all in awe of the abilities that had begun to show themselves in each of us, so when one of us made progress, it felt as if we all were moving forward.

As we had done for the last few classes, we settled into our places and waited for our teacher to begin. Maeve opened her arms in welcome and smiled. "Let's start with you," she said, pointing at me. "Tell us about this morning, Rebecca."

I shifted in my seat and sat up straighter, like a child called upon in class. "Well, I was able to do my first reading at the assembly today, and I thought it went fairly well. I read for a young woman who had lost her grandfather, and it was easier than I thought it would be. The grandfather was literally standing behind her trying to get my attention while the others were doing their readings. But..." I paused before I confessed my concerns, "Something odd is happening between him and me."

Maeve raised her brows. "You and the grandfather?"

I nodded. "I feel like I know this guy. He has shown up in my life a couple of times already. I feel like his energy is familiar, and it doesn't feel like the energy of an old man."

"That's interesting," Maeve said. "Tell me what his energy feels like."

I thought for a moment. "Well, the first couple of times, it was as if he was somehow engaged in what was happening around me, almost as if he was involved in the outcome." I described how I detected a spark of energy in my classroom that last day of school, and my feeling of his compassion, especially towards Charlie. "And then later, in my living room, when Michael and I were having the conversation about our breakup, I felt him there."

"Well, that's very curious." Maeve paused a moment to consider my words. "Why don't we go into a group meditation, and see if we can get a better sense of who this man is and what he wants?"

I smiled to myself at the changes occurring within me, because her suggestion seemed like a perfectly logical thing to do next. The four of us arranged ourselves into comfortable positions. Maeve directed us through the process of relaxation, advising us to close our eyes and take a few deep breaths. We did as she instructed, sitting in silence for a few minutes. I concentrated on my breath, imagining the oxygen coming in and out of my body. I saw nothing in my head but darkness for a while. Then, the spirit we were hunting popped into my head in brilliant color. He was not what I expected, at all.

In my head, I saw a radiant, smiling, middle-aged man. He was wearing a beige suit, well cut and hanging loose about his tall, muscular frame, with a starched white shirt and a thin black tie. He had gleaming black hair and a playful light in his eye that made me smile. He reminded me of the heroes in those old gangster movies made in the 1940s. Once I had him full in my sights, he bowed formally, as if we had just been introduced. I was delighted by his presence, but confused. This could not be the ponytailed girl's grandfather. Where was the old man? The fellow in my head looked amused by my uncertainty.

Maeve called us back from our meditations.

The three of us opened our eyes. It was time to compare notes. Tracy was the first to speak. "Wow, that was weird," she said. "You are not going to believe what I saw."

8

fter the meditation, we each described what
occurred in our quest to learn more about the
ponytailed girl's grandfather. Everybody got
something different.

"His name is Sebastian," Tracy said with certainty.

I thought to myself that the name fit him perfectly.
"How, exactly, did you get that?" I asked her.

Tracy tipped her head, rethinking the experience.
"Well, I didn't get any pictures. I just heard that name,
over and over," she said, "and when that started to get
tiring, I asked him if there was anything he wanted me
to know. I saw this really sweet-looking old man, but
he was looking at his watch, like he was late for something, and worried." She shrugged. "That's all I got."

Maeve looked over at Albert. He was rubbing his
forehead, looking serious.

"I saw a younger guy, good-looking, kind of a hot-shot. I didn't care much for his type. He was beckoning me, trying to get me to follow him. Then he started spinning into the shape of a small tornado and disappeared in a whirl." Albert lifted his hand and made a circle with his pointer finger to demonstrate.

Maeve's cat, Buster, climbed into her lap, making a soft bed out of the comforter across her legs. She scratched his ears as she thought aloud. "Hmmm. Sebastian. Young and handsome. Old and worried. Interesting." She looked over at me. "He wants something," she said. "Desperately. That's what I got."

"I saw a shattered plate and hands grabbing the pieces and gluing them together. And then I saw other hands helping him fix the plate. They were our hands," she said.

We three students stared at our teacher.

"I don't like it," Albert said, with a touch of dismay. "The guy I saw was an arrogant pretty boy. I don't think anything good can come from helping somebody like that."

Maeve smiled gently at Albert. "You have to trust, my friend, that we are getting exactly the information we need to do the work that we do. Why don't you try to spend a few minutes thinking from your heart instead of your head, and perhaps we can learn a bit more about this puzzle."

We watched as Albert sighed and closed his eyes. I imagined him drawing his attention to his heart where, as Maeve had taught us, our deepest wisdom could be found. I sensed he was lingering there on the question of the grandfather and the so-called pretty boy. After a few seconds, his face looked less worried. "Oh, I see," he said, nodding. "I just saw an image of three hearts, each cracked down the middle. I'm guessing one is his. I suppose the others are the woman and the girl."

Tracy was the first to respond. "Awww," she said, her sweet voice indicating she had already made up her mind on how we should proceed. But I had my doubts.

"I think it's too late," I said, shaking my head. "There's no way to get in touch with."

Maeve crossed her arms as she surveyed us. "That's not entirely true. We may be a century-old community, but we have cutting edge technology. We can check the security video to see where they went after the morning assembly. If they signed any waiting lists to get a reading, we can track them."

We left the class that night with our work cut out for us. I would check the security video. Tracy would attempt to obtain more information through meditation. And Albert? His job was to try to open his heart a little more and not be so suspicious and grumpy about the whole matter. It was likely he had the toughest job of all us.

As for Sebastian, he clearly had more to tell me.

He showed up in my dreams that night as his older self. I was walking down a crowded street when I passed him. He appeared about seventy, with thick white hair blowing in the wind. He moved with a graceful stride, dressed in a long, black coat with a blue scarf. He walked quickly, distractedly, and held a little girl by the hand. There was no mistaking her: she was the ponytailed girl, around age ten. As he passed me, we brushed shoulders. I felt as if I had been zapped with an electric shock.

I looked at him in surprise and our eyes locked. Then, I was literally pulled into the endless universe of those eyes, tumbling, seeming to fall without end. I felt his presence near me as gravity fell away, and I reached out wildly to grab him. When my fingers curled around his hand, he responded with a firm, strong clench, filling me with such a familiar warmth and love that I was shocked to my core.

At that, my eyes flew open, and I was lying in my bed. The disappointment I felt at the disconnection from that hand made my heart contract painfully. Lying there on that knotty old mattress, I felt as if I had landed in a deep hole. My body ached from the fall. I tried to go back to sleep, but every time I closed my eyes, I saw Sebastian as the grandfather. He was a man with wise old eyes, a man who appeared to understand how his selfish actions could break hearts into pieces — eventually, even his own.

I lay there and pondered how an old, dead guy could make me feel so...alive. I was only fifty-four-years-old and he was much older than me. Which was odd because the spirit that had shown himself the day before was far younger; and yet that younger spirit, too, was also beginning to feel familiar and dear, as if I had known him well from somewhere. Look at me, I thought, smiling as I toyed with the puzzle of Sebastian. I was consorting with dead people—and I liked it. I certainly couldn't stop now. My new friend was making it clear he needed help. I had no choice but to see what I could do.

So, after spending most of the night wide awake, tossing and turning, I got up the next morning, took a quick shower, and slipped into a yellow sundress and sandals. I walked quickly on the quiet pathways through the morning sunshine to Lily Dale's main office, which was located inside a small cottage near the front gate. A middle-aged blonde woman in a pink sweater was working at a desk, her fingers tapping on a computer keyboard. She looked up and smiled when I entered. I introduced myself and she told me her name was Ella.

I explained my predicament, which would have sounded outrageous to just about anyone outside of Lily Dale, but Ella nodded in understanding. "Well, let's see what we can find." With a few quick taps on her keyboard, she located the video footage from the preceding day, right to the moment the assembly ended. She turned her computer monitor toward me so we could watch together. We saw the crowd exit the building and I pointed out the ponytailed girl near the big doors. "That's her," I said. We watched as the girl's mother caught up with her. She put her arm around the girl and said something, and the girl nodded in reply, her sweet face looking hopeful and happy.

The two moved down the path towards the center of the village, and as they walked away from the camera, Ella exclaimed, "Oh, my gosh, look at that!" She pointed out a white circle on the videotape. It was a small round orb of light, plainly visible, moving along with the pair near the woman's shoulder, as if it were following her. I had never heard of orbs before, but Ella told me that some people believed they were evidence of spirit presences, which sometimes showed in photos or on video. She had never seen one before either and was delighted to spot one so plainly visible on the videotape.

I closed my eyes to see if I could find Sebastian in my head. He quickly appeared as his younger self. I smiled when I saw him, beguiled by the look on his face — eyebrows raised, his eyes questioning, as if I'd interrupted something, but indicating he was happy to respond to my call. I was intrigued by how easy it was to summon him. "Is that you in the orb?" I asked him silently. He pushed back some of that dark hair and nodded yes, a satisfied grin on his face, his eyes reflecting his relief at our enhanced communication.

Ella rewound the video and we watched the orb again. Now that I had seen it, I was able to detect it from the moment I spotted the girl waiting outside the assembly. It had hovered near her feet for a bit and then, when she hugged her mom, had risen and floated, barely perceptible, around their shoulders. I think it was the orb on the video that really, finally, got to me. My return to Lily Dale, my classes with Maeve, were originally just about passing time, trying somehow to find what remained of my youth, and connect with my mother and grandmother in this little community they so loved.

Like Dorothy in "The Wizard of Oz," who learned that she could magically return home with just a click of her ruby-red slippers, I was coming to believe that there were far more miracles and mystery to life than I had ever imagined. And apparently, like Dorothy, all I had to do was understand I'd had the power all along.

9

After watching the security footage with Ella, we were able to determine that the ponytailed girl and her mom had left the assembly and headed to the summer home of Gracie Fredericks. She was one of my favorite mediums. She lived in a little white cottage just off the main road, just a few houses from where I had gown up. Her yard was edged with beds of pink geraniums and impatiens and an ever-present gaggle of ceramic bunnies, squirrels, and other woodland creatures standing guard. Often, when I walked by her place as a child, I would take delight in spotting rabbits hopping around her yard until they noticed me. Then, they would freeze into position near her fake ceramic rabbits until I had passed by and they felt safe once more.

As I headed for Gracie's house, I stopped for a few moments in front of the cottage where I'd been raised.

It was vacant and shuttered now, but in my mind's eye I could see it tidy and welcoming, my grandmother in the kitchen cooking something wonderful and my mother in the yard, tending to her precious lavender bushes. While my mother believed the plant had healing properties, it was the gentle scent of the plant that since then had always reminded me of home. The lavender bushes were gone, but I resolved to get some of my own when I returned to Cleveland. Then, I corrected myself. If I returned to Cleveland. I sighed and continued my walk towards Gracie's house, just a few doors away.

Gracie was a sweet, white-haired Wiccan, whose spiritual beliefs centered on reverence for the natural world. She was one of more than a dozen or so mediums who weren't members of the two spiritualist churches on the grounds. She didn't have to be. The main requirement for living in the community was to be a certified medium, someone who had passed a series of tests to verify their skill levels and intentions. Gracie had done that years ago, quite capably, and was well respected among the assembly at Lily Dale. I walked up the pathway to her screened front porch. On a table near a few white wooden chairs was a sign-up list for people who wanted a reading that day. I was glad to see she had no appointments just then. I knocked on the door.

"Hello, my dear," she said when she pulled open the door and saw me. "Come in," her eyes sparkled, "and bring your friend."

My friend? I looked over my shoulder to see what Gracie saw. Could she see Sebastian? Odd that I couldn't see him or feel him. But when I stopped for a moment and closed my eyes to center myself, there he was. I could see him in my mind's eye as the younger version of himself, smiling like we were sharing a private joke, as if to say, "Isn't this amazing?" I shook my head; it surely was.

"Sit down," Gracie said, pointing to a couch in her living room. "Let me get you a nice glass of iced tea."

"That would be great," I replied. The inside of her home was decorated much like the outside, with more ceramic creatures, assorted bunches of wild flowers in vases, and collections of half-burned candles, thankfully unlit on this increasingly hot summer day. As she puttered around in her small kitchen, I took a seat; consciously moving to the side so there was room for Sebastian. I laughed at my own silliness and searched the room for his energy. Although I couldn't see him, I now could feel him there with me.

Gracie placed a tray with two glasses of cool tea on the coffee table. "Now, what can I do for you two?"

I leaned forward to take a glass. "So, you can see him?"

She sat down across from me. "Of course, dear. He's very handsome."

I looked around the room. Nothing. Not a spark. At least I could feel his energy and see him in my head. "Well, he came to me yesterday at assembly," I said.

"And we got in touch with him for a short time during Maeve's class last night. Then, he showed up in this weird dream I had early this morning. I was hoping you could help me talk with him."

I told her about the ponytailed girl and her mother, and how Sebastian had come to me twice before the assembly, and how he seemed to need my help to get a message to them. I explained how Ella helped me search the security video to track the mother and daughter to Gracie's house, where I was hoping they'd left some information so I could find them. She was looking past me as I talked to her. I tipped my head in wonderment. "What does he look like to you?"

"Let's just say that I can feel his energy strongly, and when I look behind my eyes, where my visual information comes to me, I can see him as clearly as I see you. Tall and handsome, the devil in his eye," she laughed. "Dark history, but a bright future, near as I can tell."

"What does he want from me?"

"Hmmm. Let's try to find out," she responded. "Let me fix my sign so guests will know that I'm not available, and then we'll go into my reading room and have a chat with him."

She got up and turned the "Welcome" sign that hung on her front porch door to read "Quiet please, reading in process." She led me into a smaller room where the shades were drawn and an air conditioner hummed. She lit a candle and sat down at a small table across from me, pressing the record app of her smartphone. It was standard procedure in Lily Dale to make an audio recording of each reading, and many of the mediums used their smartphones. Her kind eyes met mine. "Now, I'll begin with a small prayer, and then we'll proceed, okay?"

I nodded. Gracie whispered a Wiccan invocation to the "Mother of All Things," and I felt myself physically relax as she did so. Although I still wasn't certain about the God I was praying to, I was getting increasingly comfortable starting out these spiritual missions with a prayer, regardless of the deity. It was the divine intention that seemed to sooth me. Gracie folded her hands on the table, closed her eyes and found Sebastian waiting.

"There you are," she smiled. To me, she said, "I see your man, the guy in the suspenders. Black hair, blue eyes." She chuckled. "He's on his knees, begging. I can see he's sort of kidding around, because he's smiling, and yet he's serious about his mission. Clearly, he wants something, and I'm just going to wait a minute and see if he can show me what it is."

I closed my eyes and I could see him too, on his knees, imposing his full charm upon Gracie.

"Oh, my," said Gracie, placing a manicured hand over her mouth. "He wants me to channel him so he can speak to you."

My eyes widened. "Why can't he just tell us what he wants? He's certainly not having any trouble coming through."

Gracie was silent, pondering his request. "I don't know," she said. "I've never done anything like that before."

"Do you know how?" I asked.

She shrugged. "I've certainly read enough about it. I know the channel goes into a meditation and sort of moves their own consciousness aside while the spirit borrows their physical form temporarily. I don't think it's hard, especially if the channel is willing and the spirit is determined."

I, too, had heard about channeling, but only recently. Some days, when I had nothing else to do, I wandered through the Lily Dale Library stacks, trying to find answers that might help me connect with my mom. Among the books I had thumbed through were stories of the renowned channeler Edgar Cayce, who provided hundreds of hours of information about mental, spiritual, and physical health, delivered through him from a team of spirits as he meditated each day. Although Cayce was long dead, his vast collection of readings are still studied and researched at the Cayce Institute in Virginia Beach. In my library excursions, I also learned about Jane Roberts, who in the 1970s was a channel for an entity named Seth. Then, I found books on the work of another woman, Esther

Hicks, channeler of a collective of spirits who dubbed themselves Abraham, and whose lectures were enthusiastically attended by people from around the world. I was fascinated by the idea of channeling, and given my new spirit friend's insistence to be heard, I was eager to witness the experience, if Gracie was willing.

She sighed, perhaps reluctant to hand over the controls of her body, but clearly interested in seeing if she could actually channel. "I guess it's now or never," she said. "Let's give it a whirl."

Gracie explained that she was going to have to try and increase her physical and spiritual vibration through meditation. She wasn't sure how long it would take or if it could happen at all. She told me that if she felt a second's apprehension, she was likely to come quickly out of the meditation, kicking Sebastian off the channel, so to speak. She closed her eyes, took a few deep breaths and proceeded. I watched her for several minutes, wondering exactly what was happening to her. Then, her eyes fluttered open.

"Hello," said a voice that held only traces of Gracie's feminine pitch. It was as if she was speaking an octave lower than normal; she sounded like a man. She, or he, cleared her throat — as if testing the transmission. "It's nice to finally be here with you."

My heart pounded. It had happened. Gracie was channeling Sebastian. Her face seemed to take on a male's countenance, far more masculine than her ladylike features. Her eyes were squinting, the lids lowered, as if someone with powerful energy was peering out of them, and her face seemed younger and more animated than Gracie's peaceful, wizened features.

I was speechless.

Sebastian smiled gently. "Yes, I know," he said. "This is unusual. But I had to find a way to talk with you. I couldn't make myself clear through images in your head; and in your dreams, I was mired down by your subconscious. Frankly, it was working against me."

"Wow." I was still staring.

He sighed. "I am so drawn to you," he said slowly. "Since the very beginning, when I learned that you were going to meet Beth and Anne, I wanted to find you and establish a connection so that we could understand each other before you read for them. But I guess we didn't meet at a very good time."

He paused as I recalled the day I first detected Sebastian in my class and later in my home, and tipped his head to observe my reaction. "Your husband's kind of an ass, you know."

Suddenly, I found my voice. "My soon-to-be ex-husband," I corrected him.

"And rightfully so. But, let's not waste time talking about him. I don't know how long Gracie can sustain this. I really need your help."

He took my hand in his, and I felt a charge of energy when our skin touched. This was definitely not Gracie's hand. The grasp felt powerful and completely masculine. It was extraordinary. I knew I was speaking

to a dead man, but his energy was compellingly beautiful. There was no doubt in my mind that I would do
anything he asked.

"How can I help," I asked.

He continued to hold my hand as he spoke, softly
and slowly, moving his thumb against my palm. Each
time he did so, I felt a spark surge through my body. It
wasn't uncomfortable; I didn't want it to stop. I was almost embarrassed to realize that his touch was arous-
ing me in a way that I had never felt before. It felt like
my body was finally, fully coming to life.

As Sebastian and I held hands, he explained that
in his crossing over he had seen many parts of his life
that he had never considered before. He described a
life review process that allowed him to experience the
way others felt because of the choices he'd made. He
had been brokenhearted to learn of the pain he had
caused to so many, far more hurt than he would ever
have imagined. As a handsome young man, things
came so easily for him that he never thought much
about others' feelings. Doors opened because everyone
wanted to be him or be with him. Women always had
their eyes on him when he looked their way. Everything
he ever needed or wanted came to him when he was
young, and he'd valued almost none of it.

He paused, and shook his head sadly. "The people
that met me when I crossed over showed me something
that happened to Anne, my daughter, when she was
about eight. I had left her with a friend of mine. We'd

been drinking, and I went to get more whiskey. When I returned, he had her on his lap with his arms around her. She was crying and looked scared. I thought it was just because I had left her alone with him."

"I never imagined," he said, his eyes unblinking, horrified by the memory. "I never knew he had touched her in a way that...my poor little girl."

He hung his head at the end of the unfinished sentence, and the words I didn't need to hear lingered unspoken. "My wife and I broke up shortly after that. Things hadn't been good between us anyway. She made certain I didn't see her or my daughter again for a very long while." He pulled his hand away from mine and covered his face with it.

"I never knew. Watching it happen again in this odd review of my life, I could feel how scared she was and how he'd hurt her. I felt her pain, and it was a horror to me. That experience changed the course of Anne's whole life. She was never able to really trust men again...and she was never again able to trust me." He looked imploringly into my eyes. "You have to find them. You have to ask her to forgive me...help me tell Anne and Beth that I..."

In mid-sentence, he disappeared. Gracie returned to her body in what felt like a single heartbeat, and she took a deep gulp of air, like a swimmer who had been underwater too long. Both her hands were over her face, and I could see her wide eyes through splayed fingers.

"Sweet Heaven," she said.

Her return shocked me as much as Sebastian's arrival. I put my hand on my heart and took several deep breaths. "I know," I finally said. "He was fully here. Can you believe what he told me?"

She shook her head. "I don't know what he told you. I was out there," she said, pointing skyward. "I was in the most amazing place. There were spirits there. I couldn't see them but I didn't care because I felt like I was with old friends. It was so lovely. I was just floating around in this otherworldly place, but it felt just like home."

She leaned back in her chair and closed her eyes. Watching her, I saw that no trace remained of Sebastian, and to my surprise, I missed him. "What brought you back so quickly?" I asked, not wanting to sound ungrateful, but just wishing for a few more minutes of that extraordinary feeling.

She raised a hand to smooth her white hair. "I didn't want to come back, but then something pulled me back into my body. Believe me, I wasn't ready for it to be over. I was just getting started."

I told Gracie what had happened with Sebastian. I demonstrated how his hands had held mine, and told her about the sparks that moved from his energy and into my body. I explained why I had to get in touch with his daughter and granddaughter. "Do you think you could come with me to talk with them?" I asked her. "Perhaps you could bring him back, and he could talk to them himself."

"I wouldn't miss the chance to do that again." Gracie stood up from the table and went to get her notes from the session she did with Sebastian's daughter and granddaughter. I was glad to have names for them, Anne and Beth, so I could stop thinking of them as the ponytailed girl and her mother. I felt as if I knew them now and was somehow responsible for helping them. In doing so, I would get a chance to bring a little peace to Sebastian in the afterlife.

Gracie gave me the information from the waiting list that Anne had signed that day, which included their last names and Anne's email address. Afterward, I sent Anne an email message, explaining who I was, and writing that I wanted to speak to her about Sebastian. I wondered what I would do if she did not respond and decided I would try to get Gracie to channel Sebastian again. I knew he could tell me how to find them, and I wanted a chance to see him again.

Unfortunately for Sebastian and me, Gracie became unavailable to us when she received a phone call that evening from a booking agent planning a body-mind-spirit cruise. A renowned medium who had planned to attend had become ill, and the caller was looking for another accomplished medium to step in at the last minute. It was an offer Gracie could not refuse, providing her a lovely vacation and the opportunity to meet hundreds of people who could benefit from her work. We had been planning to meet the next day, but she phoned to tell me that she was leaving Lily Dale within hours to join the cruise and was unable to help me until she returned in two weeks.

"I'm so sorry," she said. "I promise we'll channel him again as soon as I get back. Can you wait for me?"

I assured her I would try, all the while knowing that I could not.

10

I had to see Sebastian again, and I could not wait two weeks. But how would I do it?

The answer came later that day after I'd spent some time in the bookstore, searching out some of the books I had found earlier on channeling and mediumship, trying to learn more. I knew I couldn't channel Sebastian, because I wanted to be present to talk to him when he came through. I would have to find someone who could channel him for me. I puzzled over the matter all day, but didn't see the answer until that night when I went to my class at Maeve's.

I walked in, and there was Albert, waiting and looking uncomfortable, as usual. He was seated on the couch in the little parlor, flipping through a magazine that Maeve had left on her coffee table, peering through the reading glasses on the ridge of his nose. His balding head made him look monkish, and his professor's demeanor often gave the impression that he was observing our class rather than participating. Yet Albert had a gentle, self-deprecating sense of humor and when he contributed to our conversations or shared a story, he had a way of casting his eyes about our little circle and making each of us feel as if our presence was important to him. I didn't know Albert very well, but I liked him. Ever since I was able to describe his wife to him during one of our first practice readings, he had been warmer toward all of us, perhaps because the class was bringing him hope that he might connect with her again. I knew exactly how he felt, given my wish to speak with my mother. And this night, I was hopeful that he had an interest in pushing the spiritual envelope a little bit further.

I sat down next to him to begin a conversation about exactly that. "Hello, Albert," I said, cheerily. He looked up at me, his intelligent face sweetly transformed by the curve of his lips as he smiled.

"How's your spirit friend?" he asked, his eyebrow raised behind his glasses.

"Funny you should ask," I said. "Gracie channeled him today. I got to talk to him and touch him. It was..." I searched for the right words, "mind blowing."

"Wow, I would like to see that. Is she planning to do that for you again?"

"No, she had to go out of town." I paused, looking into his soulful brown eyes. "That's kind of what I wanted to talk to you about."

It only took him a moment to register my intention. He shook his head. "Oh, no, I couldn't do that. I'm too new to this. I can barely explain to people why I'm taking these classes. I certainly can't do anything that crazy."

I nodded; I understood completely. It was silly of me to ask him. I don't know why I thought it made perfect sense.

Suddenly, Sebastian joined us in the room. I detected a spark of light at my right, just outside my line of sight. When I turned to look directly at it, I saw a sheer haze of undulating energy, almost undetectable. I couldn't help but smile. I closed my eyes, wondering if I could also see him. There he was inside my head, looking handsome and full of life as the younger version of himself, wearing a crisp white shirt tucked into baggy pants held up by suspenders. His arms were crossed as if he was observing the exchange between Albert and me. His head was tilted in a listening pose and his eyes were on me, waiting for my next move.

"Albert," I started again. "You don't know me very well, but we've had some fun in these classes and learned a lot. I'm hoping you can see that my intent is only to do good and help others with these experiences." I was lying only just a little bit. My intent was also seeing Sebastian again in human form. Maybe touch his hand, and indulge just one more time in the miraculous energy exchange between us. Who wouldn't want more of that?

Maeve entered the room, her last reading finished. Her eyes were bright. It must have gone well, I thought. Good, because she could help me now.

Albert turned to her. "Maeve, you are not going to believe what Rebecca wants me to do."

Maeve gave me a little motherly hug. I knew I had the advantage in this exchange, because she loved me like one of her own kids. "Rebecca," she asked seriously, despite the gleam in her eyes, "What's going on?"

I described what had happened with Gracie. As I was telling her about needing someone to channel Sebastian for me, so I could learn more about how to help his daughter and granddaughter, Tracy walked into the room. Wearing a long skirt, sleeveless cotton top, and hemp sandals, she bounced over and sat beside Albert in her usual spot. She must have heard the last of my words. Without a second's thought, she volunteered cheerily. "I'll do it!"

I breathed a sigh of relief. Of course, Tracy would do it. Why hadn't I thought of that? I looked over at Maeve. "Do you mind if we try?

Maeve considered my request. "Now?"

In my head, I saw Sebastian nodding as if the motion of his head would somehow influence the motion of mine. I smiled and nodded too. "I really need to get to the bottom of this. If there's an open window allowing us to contact him from where ever he is, I want to make sure it doesn't close before we're able to help him."

Our teacher shrugged. "I think it sounds like an interesting opportunity to test our skills and maybe learn some new ones."

Tracy clapped in delight. "Okay, how do we begin?"

Maeve thought for a moment, deciding how to proceed. "Well, we start with a prayer first," she said. "As always."

She closed her eyes and raised her face to the heavens, her words imploring her God that only spirits with the highest and best intentions might enter our circle.

I wondered nervously if her invocation would exclude my new friend, Sebastian. I checked for him in my mind's eye. He was staring solemnly at Maeve, his eyes intense, face determined.

Maeve finished her prayer, and said quietly, "Now I'm going to lead you through a meditation and when we get to a certain point, I am going to invite Sebastian into the circle. We'll see what happens."

She flipped on the CD player and the room filled with soft, meditative chanting. It sounded like angels. Behind my closed eyes, I saw Sebastian in a meditative pose, his legs crossed like a Buddhist monk, hands folded. He looked so handsome, even as he seemed to be sincerely trying to ready himself. After a few minutes of Maeve leading us through relaxation methods for deep meditation, we waited, trying to keep our minds clear and our expectations open. In my head, I watched Sebastian rise from his posture and move around our circle. He stopped at Tracy and stood behind her. My heart started beating more rapidly than suitable for meditation. My eyes were closed as I watched Sebastian trying to get into Tracy's body. His body became a swirl of energy, and moved toward the top of Tracy's head. There seemed to be some difficulty. The swirl of energy lifted away from Tracy and moved toward Albert, hovering above the professor's head. I got the sense Sebastian preferred Albert as his channel and was waiting for permission to enter Albert's body. I wondered if anyone else was feeling or seeing what I saw.

"Um, Albert," I whispered, opening my eyes to look over at the professor, "I see him by you. He seems to want to channel through you."

Albert opened one eye and peered at me. There was a look of dismay on his face, like that of an amateur at a poker game deciding whether or not to go all in. He sighed. After a long moment, he gave in. "Well, I suppose."

I smiled to myself as Maeve spoke: "Albert, if you're open to the idea, let's see if you can get a bit deeper in your meditation. Give Sebastian permission on a conscious level, and then try to get to your most peaceful, happiest place."

Albert smiled weakly. "I certainly know right where that is."

We knew, too. The place Albert always went in meditation — which he had described for us one night in class — was the Cape Cod beach where he and his wife, Julia, had spent their happiest days. I imagined he was headed there in that moment as I tried to breathe deeply in an effort to keep the energy in our circle open and accepting. It wasn't until I heard Albert clearing his throat that I dared hope we might have been successful.

"Good evening, ladies," I heard Sebastian say in a voice more clipped and enthusiastic than Albert's slow drawl.

My eyes flew open. Maeve and Tracy were already staring at Albert, who in the candlelight seemed to look suddenly like a more confident, younger and handsome man.

"Sebastian, is that you?" Maeve asked.

Sebastian nodded. "I appreciate you all being here," he said, each word pronounced deliberately as if he were getting used to Albert's vocal cords. "I don't think I have a lot of time. I'm new at this, so I'm not sure how long I can sustain the lowering of my energy to be here in this manner."

Even Maeve's eyes were wide, while Tracy looked absolutely delighted. "Welcome back!" the younger woman said. "How are you doing?"

"Well," he raised a hand to push back hair that did not exist on Albert's head, "I...feel... rather...wonderful."

He looked right at me. I would have expected a spirit's eyes to be vacant and unseeing, kind of like a ghost's might be, but Sebastian's eyes were alive in the candlelight, and they did not appear brown like

Albert's. They shone so brightly in the flickering light that they appeared almost crystal, as if they were blue. Sebastian straightened himself in Albert's body, causing as creaking noise from the straight-backed dining room chair where he sat. It was surreal, talking to a dead person in a live person's body.

I didn't know how long we had with him, so I started right in. "You've asked me to help, but I'm having trouble reaching your daughter," I said. "I don't know what to do. Is there someone else who can help you?"

"No." Sebastian shook his head. "It has to be you. There's something about you that strengthens my connection to this dimension." He began to tell his story to Maeve and Tracy, starting with his death, which he described for them as a gentle rising from his body. "It was so easy. I floated around above my body for a while but when I realized I could go anywhere I wanted to the moment I thought of it, I decided to experiment. I thought about my folks and suddenly I was at the house where I grew up. They weren't there, of course, but it was quite wonderful to see the place again."

As he paused, I looked over at Maeve and Tracy. I was happy to see that Maeve had pressed on her phone's audio recorder, and its little red light was blinking. I didn't want to forget one word of the experience.

Sebastian described how, as he wondered what to do next, he felt drawn towards a point of light that brightened as he moved towards it.

"I wasn't the least bit frightened," he said. "I felt like a kid again. There was no pain, just freedom. And then, one by one, beings began moving along with me. They were so bright I couldn't make out their faces, but I felt like I knew them. We were flying together like a squad of jet fighters when I began to see images of my life all around me."

When he stopped speaking, Albert's body went still and his eyes closed. I was afraid Sebastian had gone. Maeve leaned towards Albert to touch his hand, when his eyes flew open and we knew Sebastian was still there.

"So, it's true?" Tracy asked without missing a beat. "When we die we see everything that we did in our lives? The good and bad?"

Sebastian nodded. "Yes, unfortunately for me. I saw I could have done so much more good in my life, and the pain from the bad moments was nearly unbearable."

He described his life review and how, as he watched his life speed by, it was as if he were reliving every experience. It was wonderful to watch the times when he had been kind and compassionate, but there were many experiences that made him want to cover his eyes. "It felt like a movie was playing all around me, but I was in it. It was my life, and yet, I could see through the eyes of all of the other people and feel their feelings." He paused for a moment, and moved his jaw back and forth, as if adjusting it. "I was shown every person I'd ever met and how I'd impacted their life, good or bad."

Though he'd spoken of this when Gracie channeled him, I was still spellbound by his description of the death experience; we all were. He described how, as a young man, he'd grown accustomed to people's reactions to his good looks. It helped that he was charming and funny. Most women got a look in their eyes when they met him and he knew immediately what they wished; but he was a careless Romeo who never truly engaged with any one woman, because there was always another waiting.

It wasn't until his life review that he finally understood. He was able to feel the pain of each careless dismissal, each heartbreak, one by one. He lowered his head, staring at Albert's hands, which he wrung in Albert's lap. "It really hurt. Over and over I felt their shame, and sadness and pain from my careless use of their bodies." He opened his mouth to speak again, but no words came out. We watched in silence as he gathered his composure. "I was a very stupid man," he said sadly. "Even in my marriage, it took me a very long time to grow up, and by the time I did, I'd already lost my wife and my daughter."

"Your daughter and granddaughter love you," I said to Sebastian. "That's easy for anyone to see."

His eyes scanned each of ours, trying to make us understand. "It's going to happen again," he said. "The kind of heartbreak I inflicted on so many women...it's going to happen to Beth."

"How do you know?" asked Tracy.

He shrugged. "I just know." His eyes filled with pain as he continued, "She's drawn to a young man who is very much like I was, and he's going to break her heart like I did to so many just like her. But he's meaner than I ever was. He's going to crush her spirit, and maybe even hurt her. Badly. You have to find her before he does."

11

Sebastian started shaking his head back and forth. At first I didn't understand what he was doing, but it became clear that Albert was returning to his body. Sebastian's clear-eyed gaze dimmed, and Albert's eyes blinked and slowly focused. He seemed shocked by our faces, and a tear made its way down his cheek. Albert put his hand up to his face and touched the wetness there. Finally, he sighed. "That was incredible."

We waited in shocked silence for him to say more. He looked at each of us, "I was with her. I was with Julia. I didn't want to come back." He told us how in his meditation, he had felt it when Sebastian had entered his body. He described being able to watch the process as if from a distance away. It was a pleasant enough place to be, for a time, he said, as if he were in a dream. The areas around him were dim and non-distinct, until he heard Julia calling him. His voice was thick with emotion. "She was so beautiful. She looked even lovelier than I remember. I was able to hold her for just a moment, and her flesh felt so real.

"We talked about where she is now, and she told me she's in a place where people can do and be whatever they like. She's painting again and playing her cello," he continued, "and she is so happy. I never imagined her being somewhere that she was happy."

He pushed back his thin, graying hair, and I was amazed at the change in his demeanor. A different Albert had returned to us. This man who had been so sad and defeated was now brimming with hope-filled energy, eyes vibrant and open wide.

The very best part, he said, was their discussion about her death. "Near the end of her life, she had asked me to help her end it, to stop all the pain, and I couldn't do it," he whispered so quietly that we had to lean in to hear. Albert covered his face with his hands and broke down. "I didn't have the courage to help her. I couldn't be a part of ending her life."

We waited while he composed himself. When he finally looked up at us, he smiled weakly, clearly attempting to get a grip on his emotions so he could finish his story. "These are tears of joy," he said. He and Julia had walked through an extraordinary garden, a place, she'd told him, which some of those in spirit worked together to create. Julia, a life-long gardener, described spending hours to her heart's content, digging in the sweet, rich dirt, imagining into existence exquisite flowers that seemed to grow with abandon simply because she wished them to do so. Julia and Albert had walked down a pathway filled with giant daisies, and roses the size of beach balls. Then they came to a hanging plant with blooms that looked like enormous tulips of the most vivid blues and purples, and when Julia reached up and tipped one, it poured out a golden liquid that they could sip. The taste was like honey and it made Albert feel as if his heart had burst open with joy.

"I embraced Julia and we stood for what seemed hours, just looking into each other's eyes. She told me that her dying was incredibly blissful, that when her spirit left her body, she felt the most exquisite relief from the pain." Then, just when she began to explain to him about how he had done the exact right thing by not helping her die, but instead sitting by her and lovingly caring for her as she passed, Albert was pulled back into his body.

"It was quite a shock," he said, "trying to fit my energy back into this body. And I didn't want to come back; I wanted to stay with Julia. But I somehow knew that we would be together again soon. Our reunion was astoundingly joyful, but far too quick." He looked into Maeve's eyes. "I need to go back to her, and soon."

Our teacher straightened in her chair, surveying our little group of fledgling mediums. "Well, I think before we proceed, we should all take a couple of days to process what just happened. I want to read up on channeling and learn more...see how to prolong it if the subject wishes, or end it quickly if we don't like the way it's proceeding."

She rose and walked over to her cell phone and pressed off the audio recorder that had been running during the session. "I'll email you each a digital copy of tonight's recording and see if we can do this even better the next time. Before we reach out to Sebastian's family, I would like to be certain we are clear on how to proceed. I don't want to make things worse for his daughter and granddaughter by bungling the message."

I agreed. I stood too, and walked over to Albert as he was rising out of his chair. "You didn't ask, but I think you should know that Sebastian came through, loud and clear."

He furrowed his brow. "I hadn't even thought of Sebastian. I was so blown away by what happened to me. Did he give you the information you needed?"

I took a breath and forged ahead. "Albert, I have to ask you a favor."

He was still brimming with the powerful energy he'd absorbed from his meeting with Julia. "Anything," he replied.

"I'd like to spend a few more minutes with Sebastian," I said, feeling just a little guilty because of Maeve's request we take some time for research, but I simply could not wait two days to see Sebastian again. I didn't feel as if we had the luxury of time to "process."

"I wonder if you could find a few moments for me tomorrow, maybe after the morning assembly?" As I looked into his eyes, now so filled with hope and relief at the recent infusion of his wife's love, I thought to myself, *say yes, say yes, say yes...*

And he did. "I could come over right now, if you like. I would do anything to get back to Julia for a few minutes more."

Our eyes met, and it was as if we made a silent commitment to each other. I knew that if Albert felt as I did, one more minute was too long to wait. We said goodnight to Maeve and Tracy, and I hugged them both, thanking them for an amazing class.

Maeve seemed to sense that I was planning something, and I could tell that she wanted me to wait until we were together again. She looked deep into my eyes and said, "Rebecca, I trust your judgment, completely. But you might not want to tread into unfamiliar areas without an experienced guide. This is all too new for you. Please wait until our next class to pursue it any further."

"Albert's just walking me home," I told her. "I only want to hear more about his experience with Julia." I wasn't lying; I really did want to hear more about where Albert went when Sebastian inhabited his body. I also wanted to talk with Sebastian again, because I needed to know how to find Beth and Anne. I felt a certain urgency when I thought about them, and Sebastian had told us time was of the essence. I also wanted to feel, once more, the electricity that had passed between Sebastian and me. I wanted more of what Albert had tasted. I felt as if Sebastian could open all the doors to eternity for me, and Albert held the key. I wanted more of that, and I wanted it now.

Albert and I walked silently to my apartment. We moved through the darkness towards the garage apartment, our steps accompanied by the soft sounds of air conditioners and crickets. Lily Dale was peaceful in the evenings, but the gentle night did nothing to calm my impatient heart. Something was happening to me that I could not control. My only thought was of being with Sebastian. It wasn't sexual, it was physiological. There was something about Sebastian that made me feel like we'd been connected long before he began appearing in my life. It was as if I had just discovered that he was part of me, and I needed to be with him again to feel whole.

We got to my door and Albert stood behind me while I fumbled for my key in the darkness. "Wait," Albert said, reaching into his pants pocket. He pulled out a little flashlight and pointed it at the lock so I could see what I was doing. The light did the trick and I gratefully slid the key into the lock and turned it. The door opened, and we climbed the stairs to Maeve's guest apartment. In moments, we were standing in my little kitchen, awkwardly looking at each other, like two teenagers who had managed to find a quiet location for a first kiss. But this wasn't about us. I knew

Albert couldn't wait to get back to Julia. We both had something we needed, and I didn't want to waste another minute.

"Sit down," I told Albert, pointing to an overstuffed chair in the tiny room that was my parlor. He did as I asked, and I sat across from him. "Okay," I said, nervously, "it was fairly simple. We started with a prayer, then went into a meditation. So, let's try that again."

I said a quick and sincere prayer inviting the white light of the divine to fill the room, and asked that only spirits with the highest and best intentions be allowed to join us. We both began to meditate. I whispered to Albert, "You have to invite Sebastian's spirit again. You have to open yourself to the idea of sharing your body, just like you did before."

We breathed silently. I could barely concentrate, but I wasn't sure how much my meditative state would contribute to the success of our channeling endeavor anyway. This was really between Sebastian and Albert. I opened my eyes and watched as Albert breathed. He was not a bad-looking man, infused with this new passion to be with his wife once more. I suddenly understood how he could be a part of such a romantic love story. Sure, his hair was thinning, but it gave him a learned, monkish look, and I felt more compassionate toward him after hearing more of his painful story.

As for me, I really couldn't get a fix on my own feelings. The experience with Sebastian was nothing

I had ever prepared for or understood. That day he first appeared in my classroom, and later in my living room with Michael, was the worst day of my life, yet Sebastian's presence felt like an unexpected gift. I sat there, staring at Albert, my stomach fluttering like a schoolgirl who was waiting for her boyfriend to come back.

Albert's eyes popped open. The look that came forth from them was very un-Albert-like, smoky and intense. "Hi," Sebastian said, his voice slightly higher than Albert's, sounding younger, and more vibrant than Albert's deeper, professorial tones.

I stared at Albert's face as it transformed with the arrival of Sebastian. Somehow, the new energy made Albert's countenance seem more confident and cheerful. He looked around the little apartment, taking in the galley kitchen, the plush, purple sofa where I sat among a pile of pillows. He looked down at his hands, resting on his legs, smiled gently, and said, more a statement than a question, "Albert, again."

I responded with a half-smile. "Again," I replied. "I felt like we weren't finished that last time. Plus, Albert really wanted to give it another try."

Sebastian raised his eyebrows. "I know," he said. "I felt his energy when it returned to claim his body. It was like he was a changed man." He shook his head. Although Albert's hair was so thin, Sebastian's movement gave the impression he had a headful of hair. He lifted his hand to push it back in what I was coming to know as a habit of movement, although the hair was more energy than actuality.

"How old are you?" I asked.

He thought for a moment, then asked, "Right now?"

I nodded.

"Forty-three," he said, "my favorite age. I was finally grown up enough to have the confidence of a man, and I had some wisdom to back up my swagger. I liked everything about myself at that age. I liked the way I looked, the way my life was going. I was working to reconnect with my wife and daughter, but I liked having my freedom, and thought I knew it all. I...did... not know it all," he said with finality.

I inhaled with some surprise. "Wow, forty-three. That's young. I'm fifty-four."

He tipped his head, taking in my short dark hair, infused with streaks of gray, tufts of which pointed every which way. I watched as his eyes slowly assessed my frame, covered as it was by my purple paisley dress, my sandals tied at the ankle.

"You don't look it," he finally said, "and you surely don't feel it. You feel the same as me. But then, if we're talking the age I was when I died, then I'm about eighty-seven, so that would make me much older than you."

It was my turn to consider him. Although he was wearing Albert's clothing, a loose-hanging white cotton shirt and a pair of beige pants, Sebastian's energy seemed to bring a certain panache to the outfit. "I can see why you liked this age." I smiled. "You're kind of hot."

He chuckled, his eyes locked on mine. "You are 'hot' as well."

I wondered what to do next. "Well," I finally said, "I don't know how much time we have. I know that Albert has gone in search of Julia once more, and I don't think he'll be in a hurry to get his body back. But I also don't know how this works, so we'd better get right to it.

"Tell me how I can help your granddaughter," I said. "Help me find the words to convince her not to do what you're afraid she'll do, and tell me why you think she would listen to a stranger."

He shook his head. It felt like each time he recalled his life, he became even more aware of the impact his actions took on his wife and daughter, and now, granddaughter. "She's in love with someone just like me, only he's far worse," Sebastian said, repeating his words from earlier in the evening. "And I'm going to have to watch the painful destruction of the only person who knew me and loved me in my life for who I was."

I told Sebastian that I had emailed Anne, but that unless she replied, I wouldn't know how to find his granddaughter.

He frowned and tried to describe the building where she lived in the city's college district. I had taken a few teacher training classes at the college, so I was familiar with the area and told him that I was fairly certain that with his description, I could find her and try to warn her.

"I would be forever in your debt," he said, his voice soft, eyes gleaming.

As I looked at him, his worry touched me to the core, and I could feel the beginnings of that magnetic pull toward him. I stood from the sofa and walked the two steps to his chair. I leaned over, and took his hand. I had to touch him again. His powerful grip returned my grasp, and we stared at our hands as the energy flew between our bodies. Something unearthly flooded my being like a hose suddenly turned on at full force. We had the same thought at the same time, and I saw his eyes flicker to my open bedroom door.

"Do you think it's possible?" I whispered.

"All I know," he said, his breath ragged, "is that I sure would like to try."

12

Sebastian stood up. Our hands were still locked, and I helped him steady. He had not yet moved about in Albert's body and so I wasn't certain what might happen when he began to rise, but the power I felt from his presence seemed to multiply my own. Standing now, we faced each other. Albert was taller than me, but with Sebastian in his body, he seemed more accessible, more welcoming. Without thinking, I lifted my arms to embrace him, and his arms responded, pulling me into his chest. Everywhere our bodies touched, I felt his energy burning through my flesh like a flare gun on an ice cube. And yet, Albert's body did not belong to us. He was like a third person in the room, standing between us, sound asleep. Could we dare use Albert's body for an instrument of our pleasure?

I pushed away from Sebastian and felt the energy subside, like a plug had been pulled from a charger. It seeped from my body, hovering around me like a taunting swirl of gale force winds before disappearing. I could see Sebastian felt it, too.

"Not without Albert's permission," I said, shaking my head. Our physical union could not occur without the consent of the man whose body we required for the encounter.

We stood, an arm's length from each other, just staring into each other's eyes, until Sebastian finally nodded. "Of course," he said resolutely. "I don't know what I was thinking. We have to ask him."

His eyes widened and he pulled me to him once more. "Albert is coming back, I can feel it. I don't know if I can return to you. What if we can't make this happen again?"

As a newly minted believer in the impossible, I was the confident one. "We'll make it happen, I promise. I'll see your granddaughter and your daughter and then I'll find a way to bring you back again." I made my voice as soothing as I could. "We'll find a way, Sebastian," I whispered as I watched him disappear.

It all happened in the eyes. Sebastian's light was extinguished like a flame and suddenly I could see Albert within them. He blinked at me as he adjusted to his return. Clearly, he did not know what had just occurred between Sebastian and me. But given the look on his face, I knew he had met again with Julia.

"Welcome back," I said, smiling at Albert's expression of wonder. I knew how he felt. "Did you have a nice trip?"

Despite what had just occurred, I was awed by what was happening to all four of us—Albert and Julia, and Sebastian and me. If I couldn't be with Sebastian, at least I could hear what Albert had experienced.

"Was she there?"

He fell back onto the chair like an exhausted runner, and smiled weakly. "Yes..." He reached for his glasses, which had been tossed onto an end table nearby, and placed them on his face, his eyes magnified through the lenses. I looked to see if there was any trace of Sebastian there, and of course, there was not. But Albert, fresh from an encounter with Julia, was a consolation. He put a hand to his forehead and rubbed it with his fingers. "It's unbelievable there. I saw my parents," he said. "They were living in a cottage by a beautiful lake in the woods, just like they'd always dreamed of. They were so happy to see Julia and me. We sat and talked on their porch, while a baby deer walked right up to us and ate an apple from my hand. It was just like you might imagine Heaven to be, but it felt as real as this life. Maybe even more real."

We sat and looked at each other for a moment, contemplating his impossible words.

"I couldn't stay long," he continued. "Apparently, it's challenging to sustain the kind of frequencies needed for the living and the dead to interact. But I didn't mind returning to my body; I'm hopeful now. I'm not afraid of what's coming after this life. I know I'll be with Julia, and that we will be happy." He sat forward in his chair. I could see his vitality returning. "How about you? Did Sebastian show?"

I exhaled and began to describe what had taken place in his absence. I got all the way to the part about the embrace then I paused, trying to find just the right words. "It was amazing," I told him, "Sebastian and I have this strange connection, like we've known each other forever, throughout time. We embraced and..."

"Wait. You embraced Sebastian while he was in my body?" Albert rubbed his chin with his hand. "That must have been weird."

I laughed. "No, it wasn't weird at all. There was this electricity coursing through us. I have never felt anything like it. It was better than..."

"Sex," Albert finished for me after a moment's silence. "I know exactly what you mean," he said, "because that's just what was happening between me and Julia. Right before I came back, we were embracing, and I suddenly began to wonder if it were even possible to make love to her...but then I was pulled back into my body."

I couldn't say out loud what I was thinking, but I wondered if somehow Albert's being with Julia was connected to my ability to be with Sebastian. It didn't matter. I simply could not find the words to ask a man I hardly knew if I could borrow his body to make another man my spiritual lover. I could see that he was struggling with the same awareness.

I stood up, and cleared my throat. "It's very late, and I have to spend some time trying to figure out what's going on here," I sighed.

He nodded, and stood. "Me too. I'd better go."

I walked him to the door, and we stood there awkwardly. We embraced for a brief moment and I was not surprised to find that Albert's arms, placed lightly around me, felt entirely different than when Sebastian had drawn me to his chest in that very same body.

After he left and I locked the door behind him, I leaned against the wall and looked around my apartment, wondering if Sebastian was still there. After a few minutes of peering into the darkness, looking for flashes of his energy, I gave up. Where had Sebastian gone off to, I wondered, trying to imagine him somewhere like Albert had described. The afterlife was a mystery that mankind had wrestled since the beginning of time. And yet somehow, Sebastian and Albert and I were being given access to what appeared to be the answers to every question.

I gently rubbed my womb, where all the pain and darkness had been threatening me like a ticking time bomb. Suddenly, I was not afraid. I took a shower and dressed quickly for bed, wearing my prettiest pink silk pajamas, inexplicably feeling as if I might not be sleeping alone that night. But whatever force drew Sebastian and me together hours before, was absent as I slept.

13

When I woke the next morning, I was disappointed. There had been no dreams, and the lack of Sebastian made me feel lonely. But I had work to do. I had to find his granddaughter. According to Sebastian, Beth lived about an hour from Lily Dale, in a neighborhood popular with students near the state college in the city of Buffalo.

I looked in my closest, wondering what to wear, unable to displace the notion that I was again dressing as if I were going to be with Sebastian. I put on a pair of delicate lace underwear and the bra that matched them. Then I pulled on a soft brown T-shirt and a pair of cream-colored jeans. My beige sandals completed the outfit. I added a dab of gel to my close-cropped hair, and then messed it with my fingers to spike it a bit. I surveyed myself in the full-length mirror and decided that for a fifty-four-year-old cancer patient, I was looking remarkably red-cheeked and vibrant. I was no longer worried about the potential for recurrence that had threatened the remainder of my days. It was as if someone had lifted a corner of the celestial backdrop. I'd gotten a glimpse backstage where all the actors rushed around preparing for their roles. It was increasingly clear that death was not the final curtain. That, for me, put a whole new spin on living.

I grabbed my car keys and headed to the garage below Maeve's guest apartment, where I had stowed my Prius for the summer. It was still early and the streets of Lily Dale were quiet. As I unlocked the car door, I was surprised to see someone walking toward me from the parking lot near the front gate. It was Albert. I almost didn't recognize him. He had on a brown leather jacket and a navy blue T-shirt and jeans, and he was walking with a determined step. He waved when he saw me look up.

I could feel my heart thump a little faster. In the strangest of ways, he had become an aspect of Sebastian for me. I smiled and waved back, watching as he walked up the path to my cottage apartment. He stood before me, a little breathless. "I'm all in," he said.

"All in?" I raised my eyebrows in question. I knew in my heart he was assenting to move forward, but I didn't want to get my hopes up until I was certain.

He took my hand into both of his. "This is the most alive I've ever felt. In this wild and wonderful experiment, I am all yours for whatever you need."

My body responded before my mind did, and I felt a wave of something I can only describe as sensual energy washing over me like a gentle breeze. "Are ... you sure?"

He still held my hand. "Lady, almost by accident, you have given me the greatest gift of all," he said. "I feel at peace now. I have talked with Julia and held her, and somehow—without understanding anything—I feel like I understand everything." He put his other hand to my shoulder, and our bodies connected like two circuits of energy coupled into one full force. "Somehow, we are able to go places that most humans have never gone. I believe it involves both of us to make it happen. We have to go together, wherever it leads."

We assessed each other for a moment. It was scary and wonderful at the same time. I was glad to have a willing partner on this side of the veil. "Well, come on then," I smiled, with a nod toward the car. "We have places to go."

Albert walked around to the passenger's side and got into my Prius. I sat behind the wheel and pushed the power button. The car responded quietly. As we drove through the gates to leave Lily Dale, I stopped for a moment while several visitors crossed in front of my car. In my imagination, I could see Sebastian, and he smiled in relieved gratitude. We were going on an adventure, we three, and there was no way to predict exactly where. Most importantly, we had a young girl's life to save.

The drive was easy, mostly thruway. Albert and I chatted as I drove. He told me about Julia. They had met in the student union when they were college students. They were in the cafeteria line when they both reached for the same piece of Key lime pie. Laughing at their dilemma, because it was the last piece on the glass shelf, they agreed to share. So, they found a private table, and while Albert made a great show of measuring and slicing the dessert in half, they had a chance to get to know one another. Julia was majoring in design, and Albert in history. It took him a long time to eat that little half-piece of pie, and they had become a couple before he'd eaten the last forkful. Two years later, after graduation, she took a job as a graphic artist, and he went on for his master's degree in teaching. He eventually landed a position at the university they had attended together. They'd lived for twenty-five wonderful years in a brick townhouse in the city, decorated with Julia's colorful abstract art filling the white walls.

But their life together had been turned upside down by the car accident that stripped her of her ability to paint, and left her wheelchair bound and in constant pain. Nearly every day after, she calmly and rationally asked him to help her end her life. He never considered it, because that would be helping her leave him. Even at the end — when the injuries left her defenseless to a fatal infection that invaded her body, and she was helpless in a hospital bed in their living room — he couldn't find the guts to help her kill herself. When she finally died, his inability to spare her haunted him like a menacing shadow until he saw her again, in spirit. From the moment they had embraced, all was well once more in Albert's world, and he was very anxious to make up for lost time. He could not wait to see her again. I nodded as I drove. I also couldn't wait for him to see her again, but first Beth needed our full attention.

According to Sebastian, his granddaughter lived in a large, red brick apartment building in the center of the city, in a trendy neighborhood filled with bars, gift shops and cafes. I parked my car, and Albert and I walked over to the entrance of the building where there was a row of doorbells. I looked for Beth's name, and breathed a sigh of relief when I found it, pressing the nearby button. We waited. Just when it seemed like there would be no answer, we heard a voice over the intercom.

"Yes?" the soft female voice said, waiting for a reply.

I wasn't sure if she could see me through a security camera, but I straightened my back and leaned towards the little speaker. "I'm looking for Beth," I said.

"This is she," came the reply.

"Beth, my name is Rebecca St. Claire. I'm the medium that read for you and your mom at Lily Dale the other day. I know this sounds crazy, but I have another message for you from your grandfather."

She paused, considering my words. "And who is that with you?" she asked, confirming that we were in view of a security camera.

"This is Albert, and he's also a medium at Lily Dale. We're here to help. Can we just see you for a few minutes?"

Another pause. I heard her talk to someone in the apartment in a muffled tone.

I looked over my shoulder at Albert. He motioned me to continue. "Beth, it won't take long," I said. "May we come up?"

I heard a buzzer and grabbed the interior lobby door as it unlocked. We raced to the elevator and pushed the call button, stepping inside as the doors opened. I pressed the button to Beth's fourth floor apartment and when we arrived, I stepped out and peered down the hallway. She was waiting for us with her apartment door open, leaning against the doorframe, wearing ripped jeans and a green T-shirt. Her blonde hair hung loose around her shoulders. She looked even lovelier than when I first saw her, her crystal blue eyes framed by long, blonde lashes, but her face didn't look as carefree. I knew I had just a few minutes to explain myself, and so I launched into the reason we were there.

"Beth, I've been in contact with your grandfather again," I said, smiling weakly at the inadequacy of the words. I started again. "He's been very worried about you. He wants to get a message to you. May we come in?"

Beth looked over her shoulder toward a closed door behind her, as she considered what I had just said. She was clearly nervous about us being there.

She shrugged her thin shoulders and waved a hand, indicating we could come inside. "Okay, what's the message?"

I hesitated. "Well, that's the part that's hard to explain. He wants to talk with you himself."

Her eyebrows raised in surprise. "And how is he going to do that?"

I looked over at Albert, and her eyes followed. "Albert can channel your grandfather. He goes into a meditation and your grandfather comes through him and speaks as if he were right here in the room with us," I explained. "We'd like to show you how it's done."

Albert cleared his throat. "Beth, I know this sounds crazy. We're training to be mediums, and we're still rather confounded by how it happens. I can feel your grandfather with us now and I'd like to let him come through. Are you okay with that?"

We had her attention. She looked at Albert, and then at me. "Of course," she said suddenly, "I would love to talk to my grandfather again. Sit down, please."

Albert pulled up a wooden chair and sat on it, near the couch where Beth had sat. He took his glasses off and ran a nervous hand through his hair, the gray strands separating and revealing the shine of his balding crown. I was touched by his nervousness. It was clear he really wanted to do this. I could tell he was worried it wouldn't work this time.

"Go ahead, take a breath and relax. Let's see what happens," I said to him, trying to create a peaceful space for Albert to leave and Sebastian to arrive.

Albert closed his eyes. I watched his face as he breathed. I shouldn't have been surprised but I was, when Albert's energy began to reveal the form of a much older Sebastian, the way that Beth knew him before he died.

"Hello, doll," Sebastian said softly to Beth. "I've missed you."

She stared at Albert in stunned surprise. "Pops," she asked, "is that you?"

"In the flesh...well, sort of," Sebastian chuckled. His eyes surveyed his granddaughter with recognizable pride. "You look good, kid."

Even as an older man, his energy came through full force, and I guessed that his boyish charm never left him as he aged.

"Where are you?" she asked in wonder. "I mean... are you in Heaven?"

He shrugged. "I guess so. It's not at all what I expected." He paused and, continuing to watch her through Albert's eyes, smiled. "I hope you don't mind me dropping in like this."

She leaned forward, as if to try to get a better look at the old man. "How've you been doing?" Her brow wrinkled in concern.

He was silent for a beat. "I'm good. I really like it here. All you have to do is think of someone and you can be right by his or her side. The problem is, most people can't see me ... even you can't see me, unless I come through like this, and I really wanted to see you. I'm worried."

She tipped her head. "About what, Pops?"

His eyes moved to the door behind her. "The man you're seeing. He's going to hurt you."

Her hand went reflexively to her face. Sebastian's eyes followed her movement. "He already has," Sebastian said with conviction, "and if you don't find a way to get him out of your life, he will really harm you, much worse than before, and I can't bear to see that happen."

She smiled sadly. "He really loves me, Pops, and he kind of reminds me of you."

Sebastian spoke with urgency. I could feel our time running out. "Don't you see, that's the problem," he said in a choked whisper. "He's too much like me when I was that age, only worse. I learned my lessons. He's going to learn his at your expense."

We all startled to hear the door open behind Beth. A tall, thin young man came out of a bedroom, bare chested, pulling on his jeans. His dark hair was wild and unruly, hanging in strings to his shoulders. He smelled of perspiration, like he needed a shower. He surveyed the room and leveled his gaze at Albert and me.

"What's going on?" he asked, directing his question at Beth.

She smiled uncomfortably. "Derek," she began, and I could sense her trepidation. "These are my friends... "

Before she could finish the introductions, Sebastian glared at the young man. "You've been hitting my granddaughter," he said, his old man's voice rough with emotion. "You touch her again and I swear I'll make you regret the day you were born."

Derek looked from Sebastian to me, and back at Sebastian. He laughed uncomfortably. "What the frig is this?" he asked Beth. "Who are these people?"

Beth cleared her throat, and I imagined she was searching for the right words.

"Derek, this is... " She paused for a moment. Sebastian finished for her.

"I'm her grandfather," Sebastian said in a ragged tone, rising from his chair, "and your worst nightmare." Sebastian's old man energy stood up in Albert's body and surged at Derek. The younger man was so surprised, he didn't think to jump out of the way. The two collided and rolled to the floor. I saw Albert's arm pull back and throw a hard punch to Derek's face.

I was stunned by the turn of events. Sebastian was using Albert's hands and fists to try to beat up his granddaughter's boyfriend. I watched, stunned, before reclaiming my wits. I rushed to the two men and pulled Sebastian off of Derek but as I did, the younger man started punching and kicking Sebastian, knocking the air out of him with a swift kick to the gut. I think it was the kick that pulled Albert back into his body, but I was fairly certain I was the only one who saw Sebastian leave and Albert return. Albert was shaking his head, trying to recover from the kick. Beth was pulling on Derek's arm, trying to keep him away from Sebastian. As her eyes surveyed the older man, I couldn't see if she recognized the departure of her grandfather.

Derek did not. He jumped up from the floor, rubbing his chin where Sebastian had landed a punch, and with fierce, angry eyes, shouted at Albert and me. "Get the hell out of here!" He pointed to the door.

Albert just shook his head, clearly confused. Derek glared at me and shouted, "You get him the hell out of here."

Beth tried to calm him. "Derek, he's just trying to make sure you don't…" Her words floated like burning embers to the floor. He shoved her away and she fell against the doorframe. She looked up at him with imploring, tear-filled eyes and whispered, "Derek, no!"

Derek moved swiftly toward me, and I tried not to flinch when he came so close to my face that we were nose-to-nose. I pulled my shoulders back and glared at him. I was a second grade teacher after all, and not easily intimidated. I spoke each word slowly and deliberately. "You keep your hands off her, do you hear me?"

Albert caught on pretty quickly. He was at my side in seconds, gently pushing me away and calmly facing the angry young man. "Now, wait just a second," he said.

That was when Derek grabbed him by the front of his coat, dragged him to the door, opened it and threw Albert into the hallway. I heard Albert's shout of protest and then a thud. I was trying to see past Derek to determine whether Albert was injured, when Derek looked at me with dark eyes squinting. "Get out," he spat.

There was fear in Beth's eyes, but I knew we were helpless to do anything until she wanted to help herself. I walked out the open door and when I was safely in the hallway, I shouted back into the room, "Beth, we can help you. You know where to find us."

The door slammed in my face.

14

Albert and I drove away in silence. I closed my eyes and rubbed them with my fingers. All I could see was the fear in Beth's face. Albert just kept shaking his head in disbelief. As we drove, I filled him in on the details of what occurred while he was out of his body. I told him how Sebastian had lunged at the young man and how the kick in the gut had pulled Albert back into his body.

"Where were you?" I asked. "Were you with Julia?"

I could feel his eyes on me. He took a breath and sighed deeply. "No, I couldn't find her." He described how, when he left his body to Sebastian, he sort of floated over the room until he was pulled away through a tunnel of sorts and how, when he came to the end, he was in an exquisite park filled with colors so rich and beautiful they were nearly indescribable. In the distance, he could sense Julia waiting for him, but he couldn't see her. Instead, to his surprise, he came across Sebastian's young self, the guy in the suspenders with the beautiful face and slicked back, dark hair. "I was surprised to see him, because I knew he was with you, in my body, but he explained that I was seeing an aspect of himself and that he had arranged to meet with me while Beth talked with his older self, so he could help me understand why he needs our help."

I rubbed my forehead. Two Sebastians, an aspect of Sebastian? That was something interesting to consider.

"That man, Derek, is going to kill Beth," Albert told me. "Sebastian feels responsible for Beth's attraction to Derek. If anything happened to her, it would just be more darkness for Anne. Neither woman deserves that kind of pain."

We drove in silence for a while. It was a beautiful summer day, the air filled with the smells of plants in full bloom and lake breezes. Yet my heart was sad. I thought about Sebastian and the undeniable love I felt toward him and now, toward even Beth and Anne. How on earth could we proceed without infuriating Derek and putting Beth in further danger?

"We have to do something," Albert said, finally.

I knew we needed more help. I couldn't call the police, because I couldn't prove that Derek had done anything. I could, however, call for help from a higher source. "Tonight, we'll ask Maeve and Tracy to help us," I said. "We can find out how to reach Derek and reign him in. I don't see how he can resist us, because we have the big guns from up there." I smiled, and pointed upward with my finger.

Albert smiled too. "Well, they're not really up there," he said. "From what I understand, they're here, all around us, but in another dimension of sorts. But definitely still here."

I thought about that. All around us. "Even better," I said. When we got back to my apartment, I asked Albert to come up for lunch. I had some grainy bread from the bakery in town and sharp cheese, which I turned into grilled sandwiches. I poured lemonade and, as we sat at the small table in my kitchen, he observed me thoughtfully as he chewed.

"I'm starting to like this Sebastian guy," he said. "I didn't at first, but I can feel him now when he's in my body. I get the sense he's a good guy."

I thought for a moment before admitting, in a blatant understatement, "I like him, too."

Suddenly, I saw Sebastian in my mind's eye. His mouth was turned up at the corner in a small smile. He bowed in humble gratitude. I felt my heart constrict in loving response.

Albert took a sip of lemonade, carefully put down his drink and looked up at me through his wire-rimmed glasses, his own eyes clear and serious. "He's here now, you know."

"Yes," I said simply. "I know."

We talked for a moment about what to do next. Would Albert take his leave and let Sebastian come into the room? We knew we needed more spiritual help and Sebastian seemed to be the man who had all the knowledge about Beth and Derek. But I had ulterior motives and felt guilty about them. I had to confess to Albert.

"This is so strange to admit," I finally said. "But I think I'm falling in love with him. We have this connection that I don't really understand, I can't even put words to it."

Albert nodded. "Sebastian told me about that. It appears you and he and I have been together for a very long time, sort of like kindred souls," he said, expanding his arms to indicate the entire universe.

I nodded, not really surprised. It made complete sense to me. "Are you and Julia kindred souls?"

He looked down at his plate, toying with the remains of his sandwich. "That's funny, because I would have thought we were. But what I'm learning out there is that this was our first lifetime together and while we fell deeply in love, we had never been connected spiritually, until now.

"Now, our souls are connected," he said with certainty. "But the odd thing is that, after sitting with Sebastian out there, I also knew my soul was connected to his and yours." We sat in silence. I could feel Sebastian waiting patiently. "Well, I'm going to head out to see if I can find Julia again. Sebastian seems to have a need for my body," he said, cheerily.

I sat straighter in my chair, my hand rising reflexively to my heart, which I felt beating faster. "Do you mind?" I asked, quietly.

"Are you kidding?" he smiled. "I'm going to meet up with Julia in a place more beautiful than anywhere I've ever been. I feel her waiting there for me. So...it's all good." He looked pointedly at me. "I am at your service, for whatever you need." He stood up and we hugged, like dear friends embracing before one takes off on a long journey. I understood we were both heading out for impossible adventures and yet each quest felt, at that moment, more real than life itself.

Albert sat down on the couch, his back straight, feet on the floor. He took off his glasses and set them on the end table. Then he began breathing deeply, relaxing himself into a meditation. I couldn't help but stare, watching Albert's gentle face with all its soft edges slowly take on the form of Sebastian's more sharply defined lines. After a moment, I could sense Sebastian's presence in the room, a powerful energy dancing like a pinball off the walls. When Albert's eyelids flew open, they revealed Sebastian's eyes, blazing with life.

Those eyes turned to me, filled with an exquisite, welcoming love. "Hello," he said simply, "I'm back."

I felt lightheaded. I knew this was a dead man. I knew what was happening could be considered wrong and possibly sinful by some. But looking into Sebastian's eyes, I felt the most holy of connections, like he had just returned from someplace far away and I had been deeply, heart-wrenchingly lonely without him. In his presence, I felt joy in its purest form.

"Hello," I breathed in response, "you're back."

He appeared to me in his younger form, the forty-something fellow with the wild dark hair, slicked back in an unruly mess. I was getting used to how the energy reformed Albert's face into Sebastian's more refined, sculpted features and gave the impression of dark hair lit with crystals. Perhaps it was just the way my eyes were able to see Sebastian, but there was no trace of Albert in my vision. Sebastian stood and held out his arms to me, and I moved into his embrace and breathed a sigh. His arms around me stirred an energy in me that was not just sensual, but intoxicating. As he pushed the strands of hair off my face, I peered into his eyes. They were so different from Albert's, which were brown and wise. Sebastian's were clear and vibrant, flecked with light like a starry sky at midnight. There was nothing I wanted to do but stand there in his arms, feeling his strength envelop me, inhaling his complete and loving acceptance of who I was, as if we had known each other forever.

We talked for hours. Sebastian told me about Heaven. He used stronger and more vivid words than Albert, perhaps because he had been there for a longer time. He described how souls arrive there and are assisted by other souls to move forward. He told me he had died gently at his daughter's home, in his favorite chair. It was a blessing far beyond what he deserved, but he had come to learn the blessings we eventually receive are so bountiful and indescribable, as to be beyond comprehension.

"I don't know exactly how it all works," he told me as we sat on the sofa, his arm around my shoulder, our faces close together. "Because the layers are revealed slowly, as if to allow us time to adjust to each step." He described how, at the beginning, his sprit had literally stepped out of his body and he'd been puzzled to see his old, empty body in the chair. "I kind of felt sympathy for the old guy. He was frail and gray-haired and wrinkled. But I felt more full of energy than when I was alive and I could travel from place to place with barely a thought. That's how I got to see Beth. I had thought, just for an instant, how sad she would be about my death and suddenly, I was there at the bedside where she lay with that awful man. He was asleep, but she was lying next to him, and I could see she'd been crying. I somehow knew that was the first time he'd hit her, because he thought she'd been flirting with a young man from one of her classes who'd texted her to ask her about some homework.

"It's odd," he said softly. "I didn't feel the kind of rage I'd have felt while in my human body. Instead, I felt such a rush of love for her and sadness over what I understood she would be experiencing. I don't know how, but I knew it was all because of her love for me and this young man's reflection of my younger, arrogant self. Only he was far worse than I ever was."

He looked at me intently. I felt my body respond as if an elevator had suddenly hit my floor. "I have never, ever hit a woman, you have to believe me," he said, his eyes searching mine.

I placed my hand on his heart. "Of course I believe you. I already know that to be the truth." I placed my head upon his shoulder and shut my eyes for a moment. "Tell me more about Heaven," I said.

"It's funny that we fear death so much." His fingers caressed my face as he spoke. "It was absolutely glorious, like stepping out of a tight shoe or walking into a cool mist on a blazing summer day. After I got over the shock of being out of my body, that body became inconsequential to me. I didn't care about it at all, I felt as if I was returning to my real self."

He told me that, after determining there was nothing he could do to help Beth, he felt a presence at his side. He couldn't see who it was, but it felt loving and reassuring. No words were exchanged, but he understood he was to follow the presence. He felt his energy drawn toward the ceiling of the room and he scrunched his shoulders, expecting impact with the plasterboard, but his spirit passed easily and quickly through the roof and out into the night sky. He was pulled forward with the trajectory of an upward fall, and then felt himself moving through a dark tunnel at a speed beyond his imagination's ability to process or even describe. He wasn't the least bit afraid because his companion, who he still could not see, offered the impression of the utmost perfection of the moment. They were joined in flight by a group of other beings, all moving so fast he couldn't make out their faces and they suddenly landed in an area that was lit by a gentle, soft light within gray cloudy mist. He could feel the presence of others gathering nearby, though he couldn't tell how many. Their energy felt to him like that of family gathering for a joyful reunion. The atmosphere was so filled with love and acceptance that he got the sense of having finally arrived home.

Then, like a movie playing around him, his life review began. Every second of every bit of his life played out around him, expanding into other visions, like the movie was playing in a multitude of dimensions. A veil of ignorance was lifted and he got the sense that his life had been a mission of sorts. It seemed he had undertaken that mission with no memory of who he was or who these loving spirits were that watched with him. As the moments of his life spun around him, he saw that every human he'd ever encountered in any way was also living out the consequences of their choices. And as their lives intermingled, they seemed woven together through a kaleidoscope of possibilities. He was aware that those standing beside him were also observing his life review, and though he could not see them, he could feel their fascination, as if they were witnessing a brilliant match of chess.

He felt a growing understanding that he had not played his match as well as he could have. Disappointment seeped into his being as he watched himself grow from a coddled young boy, so beautiful and innocent, raised with the indulgent adoration of his family, into a self-involved young man who grew accustomed to the way girls responded when he was near, all giggly and tongue-tied. He only had to choose which girl he wanted and because he never stayed with one very long, they seemed interchangeable to him. Even Victoria, the redheaded beauty he had met in his teens, who later became his wife, could never seem to break through his belief that a relationship easily attained could also be easily replaced.

As he watched his life unfold, he described for me again of being aware, for the first time, of each girl's sadness or shame from his careless disregard, as if each of their broken hearts were his. "That was very... hard to watch, and harder still to feel," he said. "I made so many mistakes and hurt so many people, especially Victoria. And then later, after my daughter Anne took me into her home, I was still working my game with her and Beth, trying to charm them into loving me. It never quite worked with Anne, but I was able to create a real relationship with Beth. It was more because of who she is, than who I was," he admitted.

"And now," he said to me, taking my hand, "for reasons I cannot understand, I am back on Earth, with the chance to make things right." He sighed. "Can you help me?" he implored and the look he gave me was one of complete surrender.

"Of course I can," I replied, lifting his hand, pressing it to my lips, and feeling the heat that radiated off his borrowed flesh. "It feels as if I was born to do that." I knew then that we were going to kiss.

In slow motion, this magnificent being, lit from within by a divine force I could not comprehend, placed his lips upon mine. It was as if a circuit had been connected. My body began to buzz, like it was filled with a million bees, creating a vibration unlike anything I had ever experienced. Before I knew it, we were standing and moving toward my bedroom, dropping clothes as we moved through the small doorway. As we embraced upon my bed and slowly began our exploration of each other, I felt no worry that my body showed the imperfections of age. Our merged bodies dissolved into the molecules that formed us, bursting into a million cosmic explosions, filling the universe with color and light and the thunderous roar of worlds colliding in joy. In our lovemaking, Sebastian and I disappeared into everything and nothing.

Finally, we lay exhausted in each other's arms. I moved to kiss his chest and was comforted by the quiet thumping of his heart. "That was the most miraculous thing I have ever experienced," I whispered. But when I looked into his face, I could see Sebastian was gone.

It was Albert who lay there with his eyes closed.

I sat bolt upright in bed, holding the sheet around me, embarrassed now, as I wondered when in our love-making had Albert reappeared. "Albert," I said, quietly. He was unresponsive, in a state that made him appear unconscious, rather than asleep. I dropped the sheet and shook him by the shoulders. "Albert," I said more sharply, hearing my voice rise in fear. No response.

It was bad enough that Sebastian had left me so quickly, but leaving me with Albert, unconscious in my bed, made me fearful that in our wild abandonment we had done something awful to the body he had been so generous to loan us for our pleasure. Regardless of the miracle of our spiritual and physical reunion, this did not feel right to me. Both Sebastian and Albert were gone, that much was clear. Sebastian had left, but Albert had not yet returned. Because I had never in my life imagined any of this was possible, I had no idea what to do.

15

There was only one person I could call. I found my cell phone on the kitchen table and dialed Maeve, hoping she wasn't in the middle of a reading or class. She picked up the phone after several rings.

"Hello, Rebecca," she said, the pleasure evident in her tone, "how are you, dear?"

I took a breath of relief that she had answered, as I hadn't begun to consider what I might do if she couldn't help me. "Maeve, I need you to come over right away. It's an emergency," I said breathlessly. I caught a glance of myself in the bedroom mirror. I was draped in a sheet, my hair was a crazy mess and my eyes looked frightened. "Can you come to my apartment?"

Without missing a beat, my mentor and lifelong friend responded, clearly hearing the panic in my tone. "Of course, dear. I'll be right there."

We hung up, and I began to hurriedly gather my things, left in a trail from the living room, trying to get my apartment in some sort of order before she arrived. How could something so glorious end so horrifically? How could I have been so thoughtless? Was any of this real? Had Albert and I been deluding ourselves? Could someone really make love with a dead man?

I dressed quickly in the T-shirt and jeans I had been wearing, and returned to Albert's side. He laid quietly, his head on my pillow, naked except for the sheet I had pulled over him. Suddenly, in my mind's eye, Sebastian reappeared. He was just standing there in my head, a bed sheet tucked around his waist. I got the sense he had appeared that way to reassure me that it was he, not Albert, who had just shared my bed. His gleaming dark eyes were soft and loving. He didn't speak, but I saw him raise his shoulders and take a deep breath, as if to remind me that if I could just center myself, if I could just breathe and release the fear that had paralyzed my whole being, I would figure out what to do. He was right. I took his cue and sat in a chair by the door, taking deep breaths and trying to calm myself. It would have been easier if Albert was conscious, but after a few breaths, I got the sense that everything would be okay. In my head, I saw Sebastian put his hand on his heart. I knew what that meant. I put a hand on my heart in response. That small action seemed to calm me and the pounding of my heart began to slow.

Maeve's knock brought me back to the room. Still feeling the presence of Sebastian, I let her in to the tiny apartment. She stood in my living room looking like Glenda the Good Witch, white hair curled softly around her face and shoulders, wearing a pretty powder blue top and matching slacks. I was so happy to see her; I grabbed her and gave her a hug. She was motherly in her response, patting my arm, and whispering, "There, there, dear. I'm here. What's the matter?"

"Maeve, I did something really stupid," I confessed, "and I need your help to fix it."

She looked at me in confusion. "I can't quite imagine what you could possibly have done that…"

I broke in before she could finish. "I slept with Sebastian." I looked at her with desperate eyes, watching her face as she tried to understand what I had just told her.

"How…?"

"I convinced Albert to channel Sebastian. And while Albert was out of his body, Sebastian and I slept together. It was more beautiful than anything I've ever experienced, mind-blowing even. But now Sebastian is gone and I can't get Albert to come back."

Maeve became very still, and pursed her lips in thought. She looked around the room. "Sebastian is not gone," she said, with certainty in her voice, "I can feel him around."

"Well, no, he's not completely gone. He's here with us, waiting to see if he can help. But, you have to help me figure out if Albert is okay. Hurry!'

When she saw Albert naked in my bed, a sheet pulled to his waist, she hurried to his side and knelt next to him, putting her head on his chest and listening for his heart. After a moment she looked at me. "His heartbeat is strong. I need to sit for a minute and ask for help from my guides on what we should do. I've never experienced anything like this before. I've never even heard of anything like this."

She sat on the bed next to Albert and closed her eyes. While she was doing that, I closed my eyes and checked Sebastian. The image I saw was of Sebastian hovering over Albert, trying to help but unable. "Go find him," I whispered to him, "and make sure he's okay. Make him come back to us."

Sebastian nodded, and like a warrior angel looked upward, raising his arms to welcome the beam of light that suddenly appeared to fill his being. He disappeared.

Buoyed by my belief that everything would be okay, but worried that I could be wrong, I moved a chair by my bed and sat beside Maeve. She was silent, listening for guidance. I also went into a meditation to see if I could track Sebastian. To my great surprise, I found him. I was at his side in energetic form, somewhere out in the ether. I looked around and saw nothing but beautiful crystalline sky and we were standing together on some sort of firm ground. I could feel soft grass beneath my bare feet. Surprised at this new state of togetherness, we embraced, and I felt every bit of Sebastian as a living, breathing being. His physique was powerful and vibrant. Our connection sent small ripples of energy through my entire being but they were familiar now and I welcomed them. Sebastian was in his younger version, dressed in his typical white shirt, suspenders and trousers, his dark hair combed neatly off his forehead. He looked beautiful, but worried.

"I'm so sorry I got you into this," he said. Before I could protest that his presence in my life was the greatest gift I'd ever received, he said firmly, "We have to find him."

I nodded. "Let's go."

I remembered what Sebastian had told me about the dimension where he resides. He said when he thought about being somewhere, he'd find himself instantly there. In a flash, we were with Albert. He was sitting in a magnificent park beneath a giant willow tree, nearly hidden beneath its protective, arching umbrella.

"Albert," I said joyfully. "You're okay!"

He looked up as if he wasn't surprised to see us and smiled peacefully. "Of course I'm okay. In fact, I'm perfect."

The beautiful woman he was with turned her eyes upon us. Her golden hair hung loose in waves to her shoulder. Her blue eyes were intelligent and filled with love.

"Are you Julia?" I asked in wonder. The woman nodded, a welcoming smile upon her face.

"I am so happy to meet you," I said and turned to Sebastian. He was staring at the couple. But it wasn't Julia he was staring at, it was Albert. The professor glowed. There was no trace of the shy, sad man. While he retained the features of his earth-bound self, his presence in this dimension radiated a captivating beauty. His skin was glowing, his eyes sparkling.

Suddenly, Maeve was beside me. I sensed her before I saw her. When I turned to look at her, she also had a glowing sheen to her appearance, which I now recognized as a transformation that occurred in this place. With Maeve there, I trusted that she would know better how to proceed. I stepped back and took Sebastian's hand as our teacher assessed Albert and Julia, sitting so blissfully beneath the willow tree. Her eyes widened as she registered the beatific glow of each of our spirits, but she quickly got down to the business at hand.

"Albert, you have to return to your body now," Maeve said. "It's not yet your time to be here. I'm not even sure how you were able to stay this long."

Albert smiled, light twinkling in his eyes. "I believe it has something to do with Sebastian's determination. He wanted to help his daughter and granddaughter and…" he looked at me and smiled like a Buddha, "he wanted to be with you." He shook his head, bemused, and placed his arm gently on Julia's shoulders. She looked at him adoringly. "Isn't it wonderful?" he asked. "Everybody wins."

Maeve looked concerned which surprised me. Nothing ever seemed to rattle my long-time friend. She said more firmly, "Albert, you have to return to your body. I do not know what might happen if you don't, but I'm worried that this little experiment might kill you."

Albert shrugged, "Honestly, I would be so happy if it did. I'm getting a miraculous preview into what comes after our lives on Earth. I want to stay here with Julia. Why would I want to be anywhere else?"

Maeve looked around at the magnificent sky that surrounded us, clouds so fluffy and close you could touch them if you wished. The willow tree we stood beneath seemed to hover protectively around us as we considered Albert's words, emerald branches gently moving about us, leaves rustling softly. "My goodness, this place is amazing," she said to him. "I don't blame you, Albert, for wanting to stay. I just don't know if you can. I also don't how long you can maintain this high frequency while you still have a body alive in our world."

Albert interrupted. "Even if I did go back into my body, after being here with Julia, I know there's only one thing that I want to do and that's to get back here to be with her. I would find a way to go as quickly as I could."

Sebastian stepped forward. "Look, Albert, I have an idea. You want to be here, and I want to be down there," he said, looking over at me. I nodded at him hopefully. "How about I use your body for a little while longer while we sort this out. I sure would like to spend more time with my granddaughter and..." he squeezed my hand as he continued, "now that Rebecca and I have found each other, I feel as if we have some unfinished business."

Maeve nodded. "That might work, and it would give us more time to explore this incredible opportunity to learn more about the connection between life and death. But I feel my own energy tiring. I'm heading back to my physical body now and we'll see what more we can accomplish from where we are."

Suddenly Maeve was gone and I, too, felt my energy depleting. It was only a matter of seconds before I was blinking and aware of coming out of my meditation, feeling the heaviness of my body and understanding for the first time why death, as I'd just seen it, felt so much more alive than life. In my meditation I was holding Sebastian's hand, and when I came back to myself, my hand felt empty.

Maeve opened her eyes, taking a slow, deep breathe, "Well, that was amazing, wasn't it?"

I looked over at Albert's body lying peacefully on my bed, breathing slowly as his autonomic nervous system did its job so that his consciousness could be at Julia's side. Sebastian had told Albert he would keep his body alive. I stared at Albert and wondered if Sebastian could do that. It was one thing for Albert to channel Sebastian, yet another for Sebastian to step into Albert's body and use it as his own. But Sebastian seemed able to do almost anything from where he now resided. Maeve and I watched as Albert's eyes fluttered open. I could see he was there, my beautiful spiritual partner, eyes fully open now and staring lovingly into mine. Sebastian stretched his arms and legs and then sat up carefully. He looked at Maeve and back at me. Then he looked down at the body he was in.

"Well...I'm back."

We both moved to his side and he looked up at us through Albert's eyes.

"First things first, we're going to have to do something about this hair," he said, sweeping back the few strands of Albert's hair the way he did with his own shining, black locks.

Maeve and I laughed, relieved to see Albert's body animated by Sebastian's spirit. For now at least, everyone was okay, sort of. Maeve became the teacher once again. She straightened her sweater before addressing us. "All right, you two, I can't say I approve of your decision-making, but you have somehow opened the door to something miraculous. While we are figuring out how to proceed, it's probably best we keep this between us. Sebastian, for the time being, you are Albert.

I expect to see you both in my class tonight. Sebastian possesses some extraordinary information that I am hoping he can share with us, which might make life a little easier for just about everyone else on the planet. As for this other thing you've been doing," she said, her eyes squinting at us in concern. "None of us really knows how this works, so please, proceed carefully, and please return Albert's body in the good condition that you found it," she admonished. She hugged me, her face filled with motherly concern.

I promised her we would be careful. When we heard the door close behind her, Sebastian put his feet on the floor, still covered to his waist by the sheet. It was crazy how much more beautiful Albert's body looked to me when I knew Sebastian was inside of it. He looked over his shoulder at me and smiled broadly.

I watched him silently. I couldn't believe that I was getting more time to be with Sebastian. Draped in the sheet, he rose from my bed and walked over to me. I could see he felt the same. He reached for my hand and I gave it to him, gratefully feeling the now familiar electricity that sparked when our bodies touched.

We forced ourselves to rest that night, for the sake of both Albert's body and my own, but I didn't sleep much for I kept opening my eyes to make sure it was Sebastian who held me in his arms. Eventually my humanness had its way and I slept a dreamless sleep. When I opened my eyes to the morning sunshine, I was surprised that my slumber had been peaceful and without the desperate imagery of past nights. Then it occurred to me, as I watched Sebastian rise quietly from my bed, that it was only because my very best dream ever, was being wide awake.

16

As Sebastian dressed in my small bathroom I could hear him moving my things about. "Razor?" he called out to me. I told him it was in the shower stall, over the soap rack. "Hairbrush?" he asked a few moments later.

Hairbrush? Albert has two strands of hair, I thought. "In the medicine cabinet."

When he came out of the bathroom, Sebastian was perfectly groomed, his face shaved and scrubbed so that his skin gleamed. He had brushed Albert's hair and slicked it back and it seemed fuller somehow. He moved in Albert's body with a graceful sensuality like a master dancer, each step powerfully and deliberately placed. From behind Albert's thick, scholarly glasses, his eyes sparkled with delight. He walked to where I sat on the couch and put his hand out to me. I took it and stood, and he draped his arms around me and pulled me close. He whispered into my ear, "This is exactly what Heaven feels like."

And I knew, somehow, that he was right. The feelings he drew from me rose with a disorienting rush of energy from my toes up through the top of my spine, and seemed to burst from the top of my head like an explosion of tiny stars. It was more mystical than sexual, as if I was somehow more connected to the divine source that gave life to every living thing. I stared into the crystalline expanse of his gaze, certain I could see into eternity. Despite Sebastian's transgressions, I could see nothing there but perfect intentions and loving energy. Sebastian had changed everything I had ever believed or understood. The experiences we'd shared had convinced me that dying was more like a magnificent adventure than a painful ending. And I knew that even if our time together was brief, I would always carry his love in my heart and it would sustain me until we met again. But in the meantime, we had work to do.

"Beth," Sebastian said, as if reading my mind. "We have to get to her, and I don't think we have much time."

"Give me two seconds to pull myself together." I moved quickly into the bathroom and pushed my short hair into place, appraising myself in the mirror. I stared at my reflection, surprised to see remnants of light emitting from within me. I looked ageless and beautiful. If we hadn't been in such a hurry to get to

Beth, I would have stared at myself for just a few more seconds to enjoy this new aspect of me. But somewhere a divine clock was ticking, and I knew there were no seconds to spare.

I moved into the kitchen and reached for my car keys on the table. Sebastian, watching me the entire time, had a wondrous look on his face. It was exactly how I felt when I looked at him. I took a deep breath and Sebastian did the same, filling his lungs with air. I watched for a moment as he enjoyed the experience of breath filling his body.

"Let's go," I said, grabbing the doorknob. He followed me as I moved out the door and down the stairs to the garage. Once we were on the road, I tried not to drive too fast, despite the urgency I felt rising within me. The plan we discussed was to get Beth outside and talk to her alone. Sebastian hoped to reveal his story to her, and tell her why he had returned to Earth. I tried to imagine the young woman understanding what I could barely understand myself, but she knew her grandfather and had loved him. So we were hoping she would trust him and the message he was trying so hard to bring to her.

I looked away from the road a second, and smiled again to see my spirit man buckled safely in a seat belt. It seemed incongruous somehow that this visitor from the afterlife was so carefully secured. But of course, it was Albert's body we were protecting, not Sebastian's. I turned my eyes back to the road. "How are you feeling?" I asked, wondering what was going on in his mind and how it must feel to somehow, miraculously, be returned to life.

"Me?" he asked. We both laughed at the sublime silliness of such a question. "Well..." he paused, thinking of a response, "Albert's body feels thick to me. It's as if I'm wearing an iron suit like those undersea divers used to wear in the old days. Instead of being attached to a hose that runs up to a ship, I feel like I am somehow attached through an invisible cord to somewhere out there," he said, pointing skyward, "and this body is very heavy to cart around. But I'm so happy to be with you and to get one last chance at righting my life, that I would endure anything. Anything," he said with finality.

I thought about that. "Do you think we're changing Beth's destiny?"

"I hope we are," he said, "but more than that, I feel I have to intervene, like this is my destiny and Anne's, and Beth's. As if I have one more opportunity to spare them any more pain and make things right."

"Could he really kill her?" I asked softly, not wanting to jar him with the horrific thought.

But clearly it had been his thought, as well. "I have seen that possible future," he said, "but it's too soon for her and will be far too painful for my daughter to bear."

I nodded, though I had a million questions that would have to wait. We had a few destinies to set straight. As we approached Beth's apartment, my stomach sank in response to a swirl of red lights. Police cars blocked the front of the building. Near the lobby door an ambulance was parked with its doors open, lights flashing. Medics were placing a stretcher into the back of it. As I parked as close as I could get to the scene, Sebastian threw open the passenger door and sprinted for the ambulance, but the medics were slamming the ambulance doors shut. I was beside him in seconds, but couldn't see Beth as the medics surrounded a body on the stretcher, administering care with urgency. Sebastian knelt on the back bumper, his hands spread across the back windows, his face filled with concern as he tried to see inside the emergency vehicle.

"Is she alive?" I asked.

He stepped down from the back of the ambulance and shook his head. "It's not her," he said. "It's him." In desperation, Sebastian turned to survey the crowd of people gathering to watch as several uniformed officers moved about the front of the building, talking amongst themselves and jotting notes on pads.

"There she is!" he shouted, pointing to Beth who was surrounded by a crowd of police officers. She was crying, her hands covering her face. Her white T-shirt was splattered in blood.

"Beth," Sebastian yelled out. The group of officers turned to see who was shouting. He broke through their circle and, before any of them could stop him, grabbed his granddaughter in a tight embrace. "You're okay, little bird," he whispered, as he held her. "It's okay, I'm here."

The young woman looked up at Sebastian, and seemed to take a second before the awareness reached her, and she recognized him as her grandfather. She pressed her face into his shirt and began to sob, her small body shaking.

After a few moments in his embrace, she raised her face to his and stared through tear-filled eyes. When she saw Albert's face, animated by her grandfather's energy, she blinked again in amazement.

"You're that guy...with her," she stammered, "but you feel like my grandfather..."

"Yes, my sweet little bird," he said, holding her close.

"We saw him threaten you. We saw the danger you were in, so we came back. I'm just sorry we were too late. I would have done anything to protect you from this," Sebastian told her, nodding towards the officers and the ambulance that held the body of her boyfriend. "What happened?" he asked her.

She looked up at her grandfather. In a choked voice, she told us that Derek's behavior towards her had been increasingly violent since he was laid off from his dishwashing job at a local diner. After Derek threw us out of the apartment, they had fought for hours. Their arguments escalated until their final battle erupted that morning, when he grabbed her arm to stop her from leaving and slapped her hard across the face. As she pulled out of his grip, he put his hands around her throat and pushed her against the kitchen counter. She'd struggled to reach something to protect herself. Just as she began to lose consciousness, her hand found the kitchen knife. "I grabbed the knife and..." she put her head against her grandfather's chest again and closed her eyes, tears falling slowly down her cheeks.

"There, there, my little one," he said, patting her back. "It's all going to be okay." Sebastian was stooped over, his arms around Beth, holding her protectively in his gentle, old man way. And as I saw this completely different version of him, I loved him even more.

An officer walked up to Beth and began asking her questions about what had occurred inside the apartment. She explained. Sebastian, who identified himself as Albert, told the officers that he was a family friend and then described what we had seen earlier of Derek's threatening nature. The officer nodded as he wrote, then flipped his notebook shut when he was finished.

"What hospital are you taking him to?" Sebastian asked.

"Mountview," the officer responded and looked at Sebastian as if assessing him. "We don't want any more trouble tonight."

"There will be no more trouble, Officer," Sebastian responded sincerely. He whispered something to Beth and she looked up at him in surprise. "You are going to have to trust me, sweet bird," he said. Then his eyes sought mine. "Can we follow the ambulance to the hospital?"

"Of course," I said, although all I wanted to do was to get Beth safely to her mom and away from her monster of a boyfriend.

Sebastian walked Beth over to my car, and I got behind the wheel while Sebastian and Beth climbed into the back. As the ambulance driver hit the siren on and took off down the street, I started my car and began to follow. We watched the medics through the window of the emergency vehicle, going through the frantic motions of trying to keep Derek alive.

I could hear Beth gasp in horror, as the reality of the situation seemed to hit her. "Oh, my God, what if I've killed him."

As I kept pace with the speeding vehicle in front of me, I heard Sebastian comfort her again. "You were just defending yourself. I am very proud of you for standing up for yourself."

"Are you really my grandfather?" she asked, her voice weak from crying. "How can that be? He's dead."

Sebastian laughed softly. "Well, yes...and no. It's a long story. I'll tell you all about it when we get to the hospital."

I pressed the gas pedal to try to keep up with the speeding ambulance. Something in me understood the urgency of being at Derek's side and I was afraid I knew exactly why.

When we reached the hospital, Sebastian told Beth to go to the ladies' room and clean herself up. "Then come and find us, but don't tell anyone who you are. If they think you're the one who hurt him, they won't let you near him," he told her, "but I want you there when he passes."

"He's going to die?" Her eyes were wide and began brimming again with tears. "How could you know that?"

I knew how he could know, but didn't say a word. I just wanted to be able to stand beside them both, no matter what happened. Beth went to the ladies' room while Sebastian found a nurse and asked about Derek. He told her we were his friends, and she directed him to a curtained area but asked us to wait outside until the hospital staff was done stabilizing him. We could see through the opening in the curtains surrounding his bed that the nurses and a young doctor were continuing where the medics had left off, moving quickly around Derek's body. I felt an urgency from his caretakers and then a nurse ran from the room. A voice came on over the loudspeaker, and I heard urgent medical shorthand that even I understood, "Code Blue." More nurses and doctors came jogging from all corners of the large noisy hospital, until they were crowded around the bed. I couldn't hear what they were saying, but I knew they were fighting for Derek's life. I looked up at Sebastian. He was watching the scene with interest, his face still bearing the grandfather energy, his cheeks and eyes a little droopier than when he was a version of his younger self, his hair less orderly upon his balding scalp.

"What's going to happen?" I asked, although I feared I already knew.

"Derek is going to die," Sebastian said calmly, "and I wanted to be here to help him pass."

"Do you think Beth is strong enough to see this?" I asked.

"I think she has to see this," he replied. We stood there, just outside the makeshift room, peering through the opening in the curtains that surrounded the gurney where Derek lay, while the hospital staff worked relentlessly to save him.

Beth came to stand beside us, her face cleaned of blood, but tears still running down her cheeks. I was worried she might be going into shock, but Sebastian was a step ahead of me. "Let's sit down over here," he said, ushering us to three metal chairs pushed against the wall near the enclosure where Derek lay. The large emergency room was so noisy that the sound of the lifesaving attempts merged with all the other chaos in the room, and we couldn't get a sense of exactly what was happening. I was able to steal a glimpse of Derek's body on the bed, jerking in response to the power of the defibrillator paddles placed against his chest. It was a noble effort by the medical staff but they were not successful. Even above the din in the emergency room, I heard the telltale beeping of the heart monitor, flat lining into a single piercing tone before someone turned down the sound.

There was a look of horror on Beth's face. "Oh, my God. Oh, my God," she kept repeating.

Sebastian placed an arm across her shoulders and pulled her close, his other hand holding tight to mine. We watched as the hospital staff went about disconnecting Derek's still body from all the cords and tubes. I saw a sheet being pulled up over his head and one of the young doctors, a woman not much older than Beth, with dark skin and braided hair, came over to where we were sitting. I could see she was rattled by the losing battle she had just helped to wage. She straightened the stethoscope that hung around her neck, and asked if we were with Derek.

When we nodded, she lowered her gaze. "I'm so sorry," she said. "We did all we could."

Beth threw her hands over her face and started weeping again.

Sebastian, completely composed, looked into the young doctor's face. "May we sit with him for a bit?"

"Of course." She walked over and pulled the drapes open slightly so we could enter. We stared at Derek's body. Beth walked over and tentatively drew back the sheet to reveal his face. "I am so sorry," she whispered to him, "so, so sorry."

She placed a hand over Derek's heart, and Sebastian placed his hand upon hers. "Actually, he's the one who is saying he's sorry," he said, gently. He pointed up to the corner of the little enclosure and nodded.

Beth and I looked up together, and then I understood. I could make out the shape of Derek's energy hovering in the corner of the little space. I could feel his uncertainty and despair. And I could feel the understanding suddenly overwhelm him, as he realized he was dead.

"I don't see anything," Beth said, her voice thick with tears, her worried eyes scanning the ceiling of the room.

Sebastian inhaled a strong breath. "Beth, look at me." He turned her to face him.

She looked into his eyes, her own filled with sorrow. "He wasn't a bad man. He had a very hard life. He never meant to hurt me, but he was always so frustrated about not being able to be the kind of success he wanted to be"

"Shhh," Sebastian said to comfort her. "Do you want to see him?"

She nodded, brushing the tears off her face with the back of her hand.

"Then do as I do." He breathed slowly and she copied him, until their chests were rising in unison. I couldn't resist mimicking Sebastian's movement as well, knowing that only by relaxing into the experience, could we find a connection to Derek's experience. As we breathed softly together, I could sense Sebastian raising his frequency, summoning the forces of the world beyond this one to allow our two dimensions to connect. In a moment, I sensed that Beth, influenced by her trust in her grandfather, was able to completely enter into the moment and I could tell she was viably relaxing. "Ok, little bird," he said. "Keep your eyes closed, but place your attention on your heart. Imagine it filling with divine light. Imagine it radiating that beautiful light, enough to fill this whole room."

Beth's face took on a glow of peacefulness and her breathing was deep and steady. I was able to feel Derek's energy as his vibration rose for his transition and my heart felt sad as I felt him understanding exactly what had just occurred.

But Sebastian, from his very different place of knowing, began to speak to the young man in a gentle tone, as if speaking to an injured animal. "Derek," he said, looking into the corner of the room where both he and I watched a barely visible mass of energy pulsate almost imperceptibly. "I know that you understand that your human form has just passed from this existence. I want to make sure you are not afraid. What you are about to experience will be the most amazing and wondrous experience of your existence," he continued, slowly and deliberately. "You are going to return to your original source in a place that many humans consider to be Heaven."

He stopped speaking to allow those words to penetrate Derek's consciousness. I pulled my eyes from the young man's energy above us and watched Sebastian, who was surrounded by what I can only describe as a sort of full-body halo. It was such a beatific emission of pure love, I was almost embarrassed to find it alluring. I wasn't sure whether Beth could see Derek's energy or not, but her tear-filled eyes upon her grandfather were wide with wonder. The moment was filled with a peaceful acceptance of the nature of living and dying. Watching Sebastian communicate with Derek, I knew that I could never be afraid of dying again.

Sebastian looked over at me, and in his gaze I saw complete and loving acknowledgement of all that I was. With his free hand he reached for mine. In his eyes I saw a tiny glint of pride in sharing this midwifery of Derek's spirit as it ascended into the place that Sebastian now called home. His eyes were on Derek's energy as he continued speaking to the dead young man.

"I know you are feeling sad and ashamed right now. I know you can now see what your bad decision-making created in your life and in the life of my granddaughter. But I want you to understand that where you are going, there will be more love than you can ever imagine." His words caught in his throat. "Derek, this place you are heading to is so beautiful, it is beyond my ability to describe. You will be able to stay for as long as you like, and heal from this harsh lifetime"

Both Beth and I stared at Sebastian. I had not yet heard him describe the place he came from in quite that way.

"You will be meeting with those who love you and they will welcome you home, and show you the ways that you can become all that you've ever dreamed." He patted Beth's hand, listening to a question we could not hear. "She's going to be fine, better than fine. She'll go on to meet a good man and she'll marry him and he will never, ever hurt her. In fact, he'll honor her in a way that you could not, and you will watch over her and her family as they move toward what lies ahead for them. In the meantime, where you are headed, you will experience nothing but joy, if you simply open your heart."

Just then, a nurse pushed open the curtains. She observed the three of us standing there in our tight little group around Derek's body and a look of sadness crossed her face. "I'm sorry," she said. "I didn't mean to disturb you. I'll come back later."

Sebastian was quiet, his head down, as though listening. I couldn't hear Derek's words, but in my heart, I knew exactly what they were.

"Beth," Sebastian said quietly to his granddaughter. "He says he can't go anywhere until you forgive him. Can you do that?"

Beth nodded. "I already have," she whispered.

With that, Sebastian looked up into the corner of the room and I felt a rush of energy in the small space, as if more spirits had come for Derek. I could feel them, but couldn't see them. There was a flurry of exuberance, much like the excitement one witnesses when a family is reunited with joyful hugs and kisses. I stared at the corner where Derek's spirit had been and could see in my mind's eye a beautiful blue sky opening, as perfect, wispy white clouds parted. Then, I felt the whoosh of departure.

Derek was gone.

It was the first time I had ever seen anyone cross over. And to my astonishment, it was exhilarating. I looked over to see Beth and Sebastian embracing. Sebastian caught my eye and pulled me into their little circle.

As the nurse came back to check on us, we knew it was time to leave. "Is there someone else I should call?" she asked.

Beth told her about Derek's parents in West Virginia and how they hadn't been in contact with their son for a long while. Beth carefully wrote their names on the chart that the nurse held and was assured by the woman that they would be notified of their son's death.

We walked down the hallway to the exit. I could not believe that such a horrific event had ended with one of the most blissful experiences of my life. I watched as Sebastian and Beth found the police officers who had been standing at the admitting desk, talking with a nurse. The officers walked toward them resolutely, but as they met in the hallway, I overheard them tell

Beth they would not be detaining her for her act of self-protection. They'd seen the bruises on her arms and the angry red marks on her neck, which had made it abundantly clear she'd fought for her life. They told her they would be contacting her if they needed further details about the attack.

I breathed a sigh of relief. I was grateful, not just for Beth's safety; but also because I had found some relief from my deepest worries. Everything I had witnessed since I'd met Sebastian pointed me toward a future of unlimited potential and joy. He was showing me that everything would turn out all right, even if death interceded, and knowing that had changed everything about the way I looked at my life. I felt fearless. I resolved that I would spend the rest of my days, however many there were, learning more about the experience of dying and doing all I could to share what I knew before my own crossing over. I reminded myself that, now that Beth was safe, my time with Sebastian could end in an instant. There was so much more I wanted to learn and so much more I wanted to experience with him. But first, we had to get Beth home to her mother. Sebastian had one more relationship to heal.

17

Beth called Anne from my cell phone in the car, and I could hear the fear and concern in her mother's voice. She told her mother simply that, "Pops was there. He helped me." I couldn't hear Anne's exact words in response, only an exclamation of disbelief coming through the phone.

Beth remained calm. "I'll tell you all about it when I get home."

We drove Beth back to her apartment so that she could retrieve some of her things and then we took her to her mother. We pulled up in front of a Cape Cod home on a quiet street in a nearby suburb. In the early evening dusk, I could see the exterior decorated by flowers and garden flags illuminated by the landscaping lights. We let Beth go inside first so she could explain to her mother what had happened. We hoped that Anne would agree to talk with Sebastian.

All was quiet for about five minutes and Sebastian and I watched the front door anxiously, waiting to see the result of the conversation taking place inside. Then Beth threw the door open wide. "Come inside, Pops." We walked into the house and I saw Anne standing in the living room, watching us warily.

She nodded at me in recognition and a small smile crossed her face, but she looked at Sebastian with skeptical eyes. Her recognition of her father occurred seconds later, despite his appearance in Albert's body. She inhaled sharply at the shock. "Dad?"

"Annie," he said, his voice breaking. She walked into his arms and the two embraced.

"I was afraid you wouldn't know me," he said, as he held her.

"Well, I probably wouldn't have, if Beth hadn't come in and told me about Derek, and how you were there for her," she replied. "I didn't really believe her until I saw you."

She pulled back and surveyed his face. Her eyes were filled with love. "I saw you in my dreams," she said. "You came to me and told me how sorry you were and how much you loved me. You were so filled with light, you looked like an angel. I found myself believing you. I was finally able to forgive you."

We spent the few hours at Annie's kitchen table, rehashing the incidents that led up to the confrontation between Beth and Derek and his death at the hospital. Beth described to her mom in detail how Sebastian had helped Derek's spirit ascend into the dimension where his healing would begin. We were silent at the end of the story and Anne stood to gather some food for us. She put on a pot of coffee and made some ham and cheese sandwiches. The comforting smell of the coffee brewing filled the kitchen as Sebastian stared at the plate of sandwiches she placed on the table. At first, he declined the food, but I reminded him that Albert had not eaten since yesterday, and Sebastian had to nourish his body.

He took a bite of his sandwich, the first food he'd eaten while in Albert's skin. He chewed thoughtfully and then swallowed. "Just the way I remember." I smiled at him as his daughter and granddaughter watched in wonder, still awestruck by his reappearance in their lives.

The inevitable questions finally came. "Pops," Beth asked. "What's it like being dead?"

Sebastian took a sip of the rich, steaming coffee. I could tell he was savoring its flavor while thinking of an answer for his granddaughter. As I watched him shape his answer, I marveled at his grandfather persona. He moved more slowly, his words more measured. The overall effect was one of a gentle, loving man at the end of his life, wizened by the years, and full of love and gratitude for those around him and all that remained of his days.

Finally, Sebastian answered, "Just after I died, I went through the whole tunnel experience we've all heard so much about. I was very surprised to discover that the tunnel wasn't just a myth that we tell each other so as not to be afraid of dying." He described for them, as he had for me, the immediate presence of someone beside him on the journey to the light, someone he could not see, but surely felt.

"Did the spirit take you to Heaven?" Beth asked.

Beth, Anne, and I were leaning forward, our elbows on the table. I had heard most of the story a couple of times now, but I wanted to hear it again.

"Well, he definitely took me somewhere, although I'm not sure that it was Heaven. This place where I went was as beautiful a place I have ever seen, but I got the idea that it was more a way station than Heaven itself. I was told it was the place where the newest arrivals come to adjust and to heal." He described once more how he was surrounded by a group of souls that he felt, but could not see, and explained that the communication took place inside his consciousness, with no spoken words exchanged. They welcomed him home as if they were family. Then he shook his head. "No, it was more than family; it was as if each of them was a piece of me, or I was a piece of them, like we were all part of the same soul." He gazed into his coffee cup. "I have never felt so loved and accepted," he said quietly. "No judgment, no lessons, just total acceptance. It was so...wonderful."

"Did you see God?" Anne asked softly.

He lifted his eyes and looked into hers, his gaze filled with love. "That's the thing, honey," he said. "I know for sure, now, that we are all made from the same divine energy that is God. But I haven't yet met God himself," he added, then corrected himself, smiling. "Or God, herself."

"And how are you doing this right now?" Anne pressed. "How are you using this other guy's body?"

"Well, it's pretty simple," he explained. "Albert didn't want to be in his body and I did. So he raised his frequency consciously, through meditation and breathing, and I lowered my frequency in the same manner, through my intent. But, I don't know how much longer I have here or whether I can come back again. So, we're going to have to say goodbye, my beautiful girls," he said. He stood and beckoned me.

"We have some work to do with Maeve," he said to me. "I've got to help Albert get safely back into his body, as I promised."

Sebastian embraced his daughter and granddaughter, his eyes filling with tears. I stood outside their little circle, appreciating the love on each face, admiring Sebastian's beautiful spirit, always so visible through Albert's form. The two women were a lovely legacy for Sebastian and I imagined that parting, when they knew he remained alive and happy somewhere in a place where they would meet again, made letting him go much easier than if they thought they might never meet again.

As Beth and Anne walked us to the car, Beth whispered to me, "I would like you to come back again soon, with or without out my grandfather. It will help us stay connected to him."

I buckled my seatbelt and hit the power button that quietly started the engine. "Either way, I'll come back," I told Beth, "I promise."

I pulled away from the curb and as we headed down the road toward Lily Dale, and I heard Sebastian yawn. He chuckled to himself. "I'd forgotten how challenging it is to be in these bodies. I was getting used to being light as a feather. Now, I feel like I have 20-pound weights on all my limbs."

I glanced over at him and my heart beat a little faster. The change was nearly imperceptible, but it was clear that he was coming through as the younger Sebastian again, the forty-five-year-old with the powerful sense of self, his edge softened by the wisdom he had gained as a spirit. "You are younger now," I said, stating the obvious.

He laughed. "Yes, I am. I was holding my grandfather energy so the girls would recognize me, but I feel stronger and more powerful when I bring my youthful self into this form."

Then he looked down at his chest and pulled at his shirt, the same plain, blue cotton button-down that Albert wore un-tucked. "I hate this guy's taste in clothes. I appreciate the loan, but I sure wish he had a better fashion sense."

I laughed, too. "When I see you in my head, you're wearing suspenders," I confessed, "and a white shirt, and wide leg pants. I must say, you wear that look really well."

"I loved that time of my life," he said wistfully. "I thought I could do anything. I was performing all over the country with my band, and we were just starting to attract attention from producers when Victoria left me." He was silent for a moment. "I was such a knucklehead. I wouldn't have wanted to be married to me either."

"Where is Victoria now?" I asked him.

"She's in senior residence near Anne's house," he said. "She made it clear long ago that she never wanted to see me again. I tried to visit her when I was living with Anne, but she closed the door in my face." He sighed, the weight of his guilt evident in his voice. "I would give anything to make it up to her, to somehow get her to forgive me."

We drove in silence for a bit. Sebastian leaned his head against the window, eyes closed. I took the opportunity to think about the changes he had brought into my life over the course of the last few days, this beautiful spirit inhabiting Albert's body. Was it just some sort of supernatural accident that he was able to take it over so completely? Now that he had shown us this could be done, could more people do the same? Had we broken through some sort of spiritual barrier? And what was this pull I felt towards him, so far beyond sexual? It was as if a part of me had been missing for a very long time, and Sebastian perfectly filled that empty space.

I never wanted this feeling of completeness to end. I wanted to live in the hereafter, with him. Maybe that's what my decreased anxiety over the return of my cancer was about. Maybe he had come to help me lose my fear of dying. I took in a sharp breath of awareness. If the cancer returned, maybe I could speed the process and spare myself the anguish of dying from the insidious disease. Now that I knew where I would be going, I was fearless.

Sebastian opened one eye, and said firmly, "No!"

I looked over at him like a child caught doing something forbidden. "I'm just imagining what it might be like," I told him.

He shook his head. "Rebecca, you do not want to hurry your life to its finish.

"It's rather like leaving before you've opened all your presents. There are so many more wonderful things that are going to happen to you in your life. You've set those things in motion already and they're all coming to you. Do you really want to miss them?"

"No," I said, sounding a little more petulant than I had planned.

"I'll tell you what," he said, "I have to go in search of Albert anyway, so I'll try to take you with me for a longer period of time. You'll be able to see what you have to look forward to and be able to understand a little better why you don't want to leave your life before it's officially over."

I nodded. Yes, I told myself. That's all I really want, a little more time. I hated the idea of being without Sebastian, but I now knew we were connected through all of eternity. If I continued to explore life after death through my work as a medium, I would always be able to communicate with him. I just wouldn't be able to touch him for a very long while. I took one hand off the steering wheel and reached over to take Sebastian's hand. He squeezed my hand tightly and we drove like that all the way home.

18

It was late when we got back to my apartment. We were both too wound up to sleep, so Sebastian sat at the kitchen table while I tidied the kitchen, loading the last of the dishes into the dishwasher and wiping the small counter. When I was done, I hung the dishrag on a rack near the stove and turned to look at him. As the early morning light began to fill the room, I could make out the aura that radiated from his body, giving off a sense of movement even when he was still. I knew then what I wanted to do with our last free hours before we met with Maeve and delivered Albert's body back to its rightful owner.

"I want to go now," I said. Sebastian tipped his head to consider my words.

"Now?" he asked. "Where?"

"I want to go where your spirit resides when it's not here in my kitchen or fighting with abusive boyfriends."

I walked over to him and reached for his hand. He stood, the chair creaking against the floor as he did.

"Take me to Heaven, Sebastian. This could be our last chance."

He threw his head back and laughed. "There is more than one way to do that," he said, pulling me close.

I knew what he meant. Our lovemaking was the most amazing experience of my life. The collision of his energy and mine was so far beyond anything I had ever experienced that I naturally wished there was time to return to my bed with Sebastian. But in the interest of forever, I wanted more than that. I knew that we did not have much time left together, and if I were ever to really experience Sebastian's Heaven before I actually met him there, this would be my time.

I led Sebastian to the couch and we sat beside each other, our bodies touching. I reached across him and flicked on my CD player. My favorite meditation disk filled the room with a lovely spiritual chant.

I explained to Sebastian about the process of meditation, which was the only way I could imagine that we might get to the afterlife together. We closed our eyes and began breathing deeply. I held his hand. If we were going anywhere, we were going together.

Perhaps it was the power of Sebastian's spirit, or perhaps it was the pairing of our energy, but it wasn't long before I felt myself being pulled out of my body. I continued to hold Sebastian's hand as tightly as I could.

I suddenly felt lightheaded and when I opened my eyes, I was floating. I looked to my right and Sebastian was there beside me, our hands still clenched together. Our ethereal bodies were misty and nearly see-through. I looked down at our earthbound physical forms, which remained deep in meditation.

The astral Sebastian at my side nodded, his eyes glowing with a playful twinkle, and said, "The final frontier...?"

I laughed at the silly Star Trek reference and nodded joyfully. "Beam me up."

There was a whooshing noise and our bodies instantly and effortlessly passed through the roof of my apartment and out into the stratosphere. I was holding my breath as we sped, slowing only when we were out past the moon and the stars, and then I understood that it was exactly as Sebastian said, indescribable with any words in our language. So, I just floated there beside him, holding tight to his hand and observing the sky from this vantage point at the edge of eternity. The stars twinkled from as far away as my eye could see. I felt connected to each and every one of the glimmering bits of light, as if their brilliance was also a part of me.

I wanted never to leave, but felt Sebastian's energy pull me gently forward. "Come on," he said, "this is nothing compared to what's coming."

I looked down at where my body should have been and was interested to see that I was exactly as I had been before, but my cells seemed to be vibrating at an increased level. I could feel my spirit animated by a gentle humming and when I looked down at my arms and legs, they glowed with tiny pinpoints of light that made every cell so beautiful I couldn't resist caressing my own wrist. I was in complete awe of me. Here in this place, I was exquisite, a creature of such perfection that I finally understood the meaning of self-love. When I looked over at Sebastian, he too gleamed with a vibrancy that made him appear divinely gorgeous, like a wingless archangel. I finally understood, looking at his magnificent spirit, that he and I were aspects of the same divine source, and the pull I felt towards Sebastian was a coming home to myself, a merging that would complete me with a satisfaction unavailable to me in my everyday world.

This is where I belonged. I knew it with certainty. I was standing next to Sebastian in this place far beyond my ability to imagine, and yet somehow I understood exactly what he had tried to describe. He had told me that everything here could change in a beat, upon my whim. So I decided to play. I imagined I was at an ocean-side beach on a sunny day, the soft breeze of a perfect temperature gently caressing my face. Before I could finish imagining the details, we were there.

Sebastian observed the change in our surroundings and looked at me, delighted. "Nice," he said, in admiration of my quick understanding.

We stepped through the soft sand to the water, where waves tickled our feet as they swept the shore. A stone's throw from the beach, I saw beautiful dolphins gleaming in the sunlight, leaping through the waves, playing with each other and nodding in our direction, as if urging us to join their game. Of course there would be dolphins here; I had always adored dolphins with their great intelligence and exuberance. I laughed as I felt their energy, so playful and full of welcoming acceptance, their clicking sounds offering a loving hello. I looked out farther out on the horizon and my eyes widened with delight at the sight of giant, black and white whales breaking the surface in joyful leaps. I gasped at their majesty and knew with certainty that they too had come to welcome us.

So, I thought, this was Heaven. I was getting a personal tour of a place humans had wondered and dreamed about since mankind became aware of itself. Surely, if others knew about this place, wouldn't that change the way they went about their lives? I wanted to ponder that idea, but I didn't feel like I had time for existential contemplation.

"We have to find Albert," I said to Sebastian.

He had been watching the sea creatures, enthralled as I was by their antics, a wide, boyish smile upon his face. "I like your ocean. It's magnificent," he said, as if I created it myself.

I smiled back. "Yes, it's wonderful," I agreed. "I already don't want to leave," I said, finally understanding why people who've come back from death always admit that it was very hard to return to their bodies. I had never dreamed there was such beauty anywhere.

The understandings kept coming to me, one after another with breathtaking speed. Life was the adventure. That's why we choose to take on human form. It was like traveling to some wild and yet wonderful colony where all who came to experience it had deliberately chosen to test and enhance their skills. Certainly, human life was fraught with challenges, but those who chose to take the dare were rewarded with knowing they had enhanced their soul-wisdom by experiencing a wild world that rippled with conundrums. Win or lose, there was only triumph in undertaking the Earth school. The reward was a Heaven of our own design.

"Do you think life is a game?" I asked Sebastian, as he watched the sea creatures frolic.

Sebastian pointed several yards out into the ocean, where a gleaming, slick-skinned blue dolphin leapt. It spun several times in the air before falling with a splash, issuing a triumphant series of clicks and whistles.

"I think," he said, "that when you are faced with all the darkness and sadness of human existence, it's disrespectful to call it a game." He shook his head. "The words to which we have access cannot begin to cover what really occurs." His brow furrowed as he considered how to express himself. "It's like a blessing really, to have a life on Earth. Like going off to college to get an advanced degree. But within each life, there is no way to understand our skills unless we have an opportunity to test them, and no way to grow our wisdom until we face impossible challenges and experience the results of our choices."

"Why can't we just stay here and make choices?" I wondered.

"Well, we can, but they don't have the same level of urgency," he explained.

He stopped speaking and took in a breath. "Look at that." He pointed at the ocean.

On the horizon, I saw a weathered old sailing ship. It seemed out of place among the perfection that surrounded us. There were men leaning over the sides, shouting at each other in a language I didn't understand. Suddenly, several picked up guns and began firing over the edge of the boat into the pods of whales that had been following the ship. Bullets ripped into gleaming black and white bodies, and red blood began to pool around the pods. The whales called out to each other in ear-piercing squeals of anguish. The men were shouting, running back and forth on the deck and firing their weapons in an unrelenting storm of hellfire.

I watched in horror, unable to believe what I was seeing. Something had gone wrong, this could not be happening in Heaven. Perhaps I'd caused this somehow, with my imaginings? "Oh, my God, Sebastian, we have to do something," I screamed over the noise.

"We are doing something," he said patiently. "Just watch."

The massacre continued until all the whales were dead. The men on the ship embraced and cheered. I could not believe they were so happy over the killing of such exquisite creatures. I was certainly not in Heaven. Such things could never happen there. The horrifying demonstration of cruelty made me think of all the unhappiness such violence caused in my world. Tears rolled down my cheeks. I started feeling hopeless, not just about the life I knew I would be returning to, but this life I would be heading toward.

Sebastian, who had been intently watching the men on the boat, turned to me and saw me crying. His face became alarmed. "Oh, no, Rebecca, don't cry. I'm so sorry. It wasn't real. It was just a demonstration and I guess it kind of got out of hand. Here, let me show you..."

He waved to the men on the boat and one of the taller sailors, holding a rifle, waved back. The man lowered his weapon and shouted something to the other men, and they all gathered in a group near the railing. In a moment, their hats were off, and I could see their faces. Their bodies glistened in the sunlight the way that Sebastian's had. They bowed to us with proud gentility, like actors after a performance. Sebastian waved his hand and the whales came back to life, like kindergarten children awakening from their naps. The pools of red disappeared, restoring the clear, diamond sheen of the ocean water, and the whales returned to their water play, seemingly energized by what had been a nightmare to me. As the ship sailed off into the distance, followed by the dancing pod of whales, the dolphins returned and joined in the parade. We watched until they all became small dark bumps in the distance, and then Sebastian turned to me with an expression of triumph.

"It's Heaven," he said with a shrug. "There's nothing scary here, nobody gets hurt, and nobody has problems that are hard to solve. If we always stayed in Heaven, it would be hard to actually learn anything. We could never test our theories or enjoy the triumph of getting stronger, faster or smarter. It would be like having a Ferrari and never getting to see how fast it went."

We walked the seashore as I considered this. "I was so afraid," I told him. "And so horrified by those men who were killing the whales. I hated that. How could that happen here?"

He stopped and pulled me close to him. "And yet," he whispered in my ear, "it was nothing but a little show, presented with endearing realism by our friends in the ocean. Pretty convincing, right?"

I leaned my head against his shoulder, trying to appreciate what I had just seen. "Do not ever do that to me again, okay?"

He pulled me closer and whispered, "I promise."

We stood there for what felt like a long time as I settled down from my introduction to Sebastian's world. "So, nothing bad ever happens here?"

He thought. "Well, yes, it does, but you have to think it into existence, both good and bad. Those who come with their unshakeable beliefs in a certain kind of afterlife experience just what they believe until they eventually understand there is far more here. And those who believe they belong in hell experience every bit of the devil, until they understand they can think themselves out of the flames and into the light."

I nodded, trying to understand but content to be in Sebastian's arms, standing at the now-peaceful shoreline, the gulls swooping and soaring. I lifted my face to his, and saw him staring down at me. All I could focus upon were his lips, soft and inviting. Sebastian leaned in for a kiss and when our lips met, I felt the start of a humming sensation in my body. It moved into me from his lips to mine and through my whole body, out to my arms and legs, and circling back into Sebastian. It was sensual and beautiful, and seemed to increase in speed as we kissed until it felt as if we would explode from the microscopic earthquakes that were rippling through us, faster and faster. Then we did explode, our merged bodies tearing into a billion stars that blasted into the stratosphere. The world went dark, filled only with twinkling colors so vibrant and beautiful I had no words to name them.

We stood there, still holding each other, but without our bodies. I could not see Sebastian, but I felt him pressed against me at my side and was surprised to find that I was just as happy and content to feel him there, even though I could not see him.

He laughed with childlike delight and it sounded like perfect music. Then he said, "So...that was sex. In Heaven."

I laughed, too. What had just occurred between us had resulted from a chaste kiss. It was a most extraordinary alchemy of love and energy, but I could also see where spirits might like to descend into the earth school on occasion, for a more visceral exploration of the secrets of the human body.

Suddenly, I felt the presence of another person, as if someone had just joined us. Sebastian recognized the energy immediately and in his welcoming response I could feel the emotions passing quickly between him and this being, a deep love woven within their wordless greeting.

As we floated around in a darkness infused by billions of glittering lights, I began to notice that the energy of this being also felt familiar to me. Without words, it indicated how happy it was to see me. In response, I felt elation, as if I were having a reunion with someone I had known for a very long time. The being communicated that it was time for me to leave this place, but that before I left, I was to be shown something more.

We turned our attention to the vast sky, where images began appearing. They were pictures of my life. As they swirled and spun about, each became animated and revealed its contents, replaying snippets of my existence as real as if they were happening for the first time. I watched myself as an eight-year-old, dark pigtails bobbing, climbing a giant oak in my backyard with several of my friends. Once at the top, we wouldn't let a slender, awkward-looking boy climb up to join us. I felt his shame and rejection as he put his head down and walked away while we shouted for him to leave. We were just children, but I ached for the boy and wondered how I could have been so cruel. The picture slipped away and was replaced by me, just a little older, in the boy's backyard, talking with him as he poked around in the dirt with a stick, his head down again, but listening intently. Although I hadn't remembered the scene, I must have gone to see him after the incident in the tree. I was encouraging him to come and play in my yard, where I was trying to build a fort. I could feel his excitement as he responded enthusiastically and stood up. As we walked away, I felt relief that he had accepted my apology. I remembered we were friends for a short time until he moved away.

And then, as I stared at the brown-haired boy's head, I realized who he was. Albert.

In a succession so rapid I could barely make out what I was watching, the images flashed through what seemed like hundreds of lifetimes, where either

Sebastian or Albert had been at my side, or were somehow present in my life. It was dizzying, visual time travel, and I could only make out a few times and places, like an Irish cottage in Donegal, where Sebastian was my husband, a giant of a man with wild, curly red hair, and Albert was my son, an adored and beautiful dark-eyed lad who cared lovingly for the animals we were raising on our small farm. The images flipped and there we were again, in some sort of Renaissance period, with me in long, well-worn skirts, with Albert as my devoted husband and Sebastian as the local green grocer who would slip extra peaches into the bag for me. More time passed like lightning. We each took a different role in every life, and sometimes I was a man and Albert or Sebastian were women. Sometimes we were deep within each other's lives, and sometimes we appeared just on the edges, playing brief but important roles in the other's stories. But we were always together.

As quickly as all the images passed, I vainly attempted to remember every one, like a student trying to take notes in a class far past her ability to comprehend. I knew I wouldn't be able to remember it all, but hoped I could remember some of it. Because clearly, Sebastian and Albert and I had formed a sort of bond long ago, which resulted in us spending all of our lives together in some form. A soul group. That's what I heard as I pondered what I was seeing. We were aspects of the same soul, learning together for the sheer joy of it.

I felt Sebastian beside me, understanding exactly as I did. Albert was as much a part of us as we were of each other. I was filled with a need to go find him, and I somehow understood that Sebastian felt the same. But it was not to be. Clearly, some eternal time clock had been set regarding this miraculous visit to the afterlife, and I could feel it ticking down to its last seconds. I was still unable to see the being that stood so lovingly next to us, but I felt its concern about what would come next. I realized that Sebastian might not be able to return with me.

The wordless message I heard back affirmed my fears. It would be best if Sebastian stayed in this place. Too much connection to the world where humans dwelled took precious time away from a spirit's ability to learn from the lifetime just past. Our loving guide wanted Sebastian to be looking forward, not backward. And despite our connection, which now felt unbreakable to me, it was time for Sebastian to return to the work of his spiritual growth. We were still floating around in the twinkling darkness without bodies. I decided that if I had to leave, I wanted to see Sebastian in human form just a few more moments.

Before I could form the question, I was back in my body with a whoosh and a thunk. It felt like I hit a brick of cement. My eyes flew open. I turned to see that Albert's body was still in meditation, seated next to mine. I just wasn't sure who was residing within it.

"Sebastian," I whispered. "Are you there?"

I saw his body jostle slightly, as if refilled with a burst of air. His eyes opened and blinked three times. As he turned his face to me, I could see by the twinkle in them that I still had Sebastian. I had asked for a few more minutes and it appeared that I received them. But how long were minutes in divine time?

I turned to him, and said, "We don't have much more time to be together... "

Sebastian nodded, never taking his eyes off mine. "Rebecca, we will always be together, just not always in physical form."

He rose and took my hand, and I stood up beside him. I felt dizzy from the quick return to my physical form and welcomed his stability. He pulled me close and we embraced, holding each other tightly. I rested my head on his shoulder and heard the thump of Albert's heart beneath my cheek.

"I would have never thought that I could be connected to Albert in any way," he whispered. "The man has such miserable taste in clothes," he chuckled, "but I don't think I can ever repay him for the loan of his..." he looked down at Albert's body and smiled, "...limbs."

As we pulled apart, I still felt wobbly and Sebastian noticed me wavering. He silently pulled me into the bedroom and helped me lie down upon the bed.

I lifted my arms to him. He was beside me in an instant and took me in his arms once more.

19

There we were, in my bed again. It was inevitable that I would reach for him, and he would reach for me. Soon we were undressed and gently touching each other's bodies. "You are so beautiful," Sebastian breathed. "Your energy is pulsating off your flesh in exquisite shades of pink and purple," he said, pulling away from me and squinting to get a better view.

I laughed out loud at that. I was delighted I possessed a quality that could put that look in his eyes. "My energy has been astoundingly refreshed by our visit to your world," I said, squinting, too, to see if I could get a glimpse of his earthly sheen. When I focused on Sebastian's aura, it was breathtaking, an emission of light that one might expect from a saint or an angel, surrounding his frame like a soft halo. It was intensely alluring.

We made love then, in the way that men and women have been coupling on earth since the beginning of time, and the now familiar vibrations picked up speed until our energies merged completely. Once again we were pulsating as one being. Then, an explosion occurred like a nuclear blast and I ceased to exist for a moment in time, located in a billion bits of rainbow-colored fireworks that hurtled towards the sky until their propulsion was exhausted and they fell gently back to earth. For one moment, everything was silent perfection.

"Sebastian," I whispered, more a prayer of gratitude than to call out his name.

"Rebecca?" came the horrified reply.

Albert had returned to his body and I, who had so recently exploded and was now depleted, froze as if caught doing a very bad deed. We both lay there for a moment, trying to comprehend what had happened. Where moments before there had been a nuclear level of heat and vibrating energy in a room filled with golden light, there was now nothing but a chill invading my naked limbs and the stream of sun beams as the morning sun began to rise.

It took Albert a moment to determine where he was and whether or not he was dreaming. I was lying at his side and he turned his head to look into my eyes. I was struck by the difference between Sebastian's gaze, and Albert's. As the rightful owner of those eyes repossessed them, I could see Albert looking out at me, the brown of his irises restored and the shocked look within them reminding me of his gentlemanly nature.

Thankfully, I didn't see horror there; so much as I saw his own discomfort and uncertainty. As he pulled slowly away from me, I felt the last bit of attachment to Sebastian withdrawn and, despite Albert's presence, was left feeling utterly alone. I quickly rose from the bed and grabbed my robe from the bedpost. Wrapping it around me, I tried to think of something to say to help him make sense of it all. But how could I offer him words that made sense when none of this made sense? He had given us permission to use his body, but I knew he never imagined he'd be a part of our love-making. Nor did I.

"Albert, I..." I pushed my disheveled hair away from my face. But, there was nothing to say.

Albert sat up, pulled the sheet around his waist and put his feet on the floor, his head bent, and I could see he was trying to compose himself. When he raised his eyes to look at me again, his gaze was gentle, lit amber by the slender rays of the rising sun, flitting through my window shades. I watched as he looked about for his glasses. I reached for them on the bedside table and handed them to him. He put them on and, even without his clothes, the glasses restored a bit of his professorial dignity.

"Rebecca," he said slowly, "I don't know what just happened, but I was somewhere amazing with Julia, and we were talking about something really important.

I don't quite remember exactly what, but I was so happy and peaceful. Then something started pulling me away from her. I reached out for her," he said, raising his arms straight toward me to show me how he had reached for his dead wife, "and we embraced, and held each other as hard as we could. But then she was gone, and I was hurtling back through time or space."

He stopped and took a breath. "The next thing I know, I'm slammed back into my body, and when I open my eyes, we...you...and I, are... " He looked up at me, his eyes magnified by the strong lenses of his glasses.

I sat down on a chair next to the bed, feeling faint, and tried to explain. "I'm sorry," I said, putting a hand on his shoulder. "You must feel so violated."

"No," he said, looking away. "Violated is not the word I would use. Stunned, perhaps?" His lips turned up at the corners, and smiled wryly. "I'm a man. Making love to a beautiful woman is something we always enjoy, no matter how it comes about. I was just surprised."

Beautiful. Albert called me beautiful. Now I was surprised. I could feel myself blushing.

"Do you know where my clothes are?" he asked, a question that returned my attention to our state of undress.

I looked about my room and was reminded of the rush that Sebastian and I had been in, and the evidence of that was bits of clothes strewn about my bedroom floor. I began picking up the pieces and found

Albert's underwear, pants, and the shirt he'd been wearing that Sebastian so disliked. I noticed that as Albert dressed, his body didn't wear the clothes in the same manner as Sebastian. Albert's shoulders were a little more stooped, and he didn't have Sebastian's natural boldness as he moved. I was surprised to feel sweet affection towards the wearer of the shirt, regardless; for I now knew both men had an important role in my current miracle. I wanted to tell Albert about our connection with Sebastian, and how we three had each been together over the course of many lives. I wondered if he already knew.

As he finished dressing and moved towards the door, I tried to stop him. "Albert, there's one more thing..." But he looked over his shoulder and appraised me with serious brown eyes.

"Rebecca, I'm sorry. This is all too much for me to take in. I need to spend some time getting my thoughts together. I'd like to try to remember what Julia and I were saying to each other. It seemed very important. I promise I'll call you soon, but for now, I have to leave."

With that, he was out the door, and my words hung, unspoken, in the room. I slowly began to straighten the disarray in my bedroom, but couldn't seem to square the chaos in my heart. Where had I just been with Sebastian? Was it Heaven? It had felt so real while we were there, far more real than life itself, almost as if life on Earth was a dream and out there, where Sebastian lived, was reality.

But what was out there was impossible. It was an unformed, unshaped dimension where people seemed to be conscious on a whole other level, able to move without bodies, but so much more vibrant and present than anything I had ever experienced. And yet, right now this all felt so real, too. The experience of Albert's waking in the midst of our lovemaking was as real as anything that ever happened to me. Our hearts continued to beat against each other's flesh, our souls still felt mysteriously entwined, but the reality was that we two were naked in my bed, and neither of us had intended for that to occur.

I had made a bit of a mess of things. This was clearly why Maeve had expressed such apprehension after our last class, and why she watched me with worried eyes as I'd left her home with Albert. She knew that I was not going to wait for her, and she knew that was not a good idea. Maeve? At the thought of my teacher and mentor, my attention was immediately diverted to the clock where, upon my glance, real time reminded me we had a classed scheduled for later that day. I wondered whether Albert would join us and I hoped that he would. There was much to talk about, and certainly, much more to learn.

I threw on a pair of black yoga pants and a long, drapey, purple T-shirt, and puffed my hair with my fingertips, intending to head to the library for more research. When I looked into the mirror, I peered into my eyes, trying to see if I looked any different after my voyage to the beyond with Sebastian. But, no. There I was. Still fifty-four-year-old Rebecca St. Claire, showing signs of the wear and tear of my lifetime of experience. And yet, if I looked carefully, I could see a hint of a sparkle in those eyes, and I had to agree with Albert. I did look kind of beautiful.

20

After a few hours at the library and a long and lovely nap, I walked down the steps of my apartment, heading to Maeve's door and thinking about how much I had changed in the few weeks since I'd come back to the place of my childhood. It was as if I were evolving into a completely new version of myself. Sebastian and Albert had allowed me to explore the idea that life is just a segment of an endless and incredible existence, just when I thought there was nothing more to come. I was a student again, surrounded by extraordinary souls who were learning right along with me and despite what had just occurred with Albert, I couldn't recall ever feeling more hopeful.

When I walked into Maeve's parlor, Tracy was already there, sitting across from Maeve on an ottoman, and the two were chatting with a third woman I didn't recognize. She was slender and tall, with close-cropped white hair. I couldn't quite get a fix on her age because her eyes were so youthful, despite the wrinkles that lined her face. Maeve looked up at me. "Ah, Rebecca. I'd like you to meet Evelyn Morgan. She's an old friend, and I'm hoping she can help us learn more about the experience you are having with Albert."

Albert. I had promised her we would be careful, but we weren't, and now I didn't know if he would come back to our class. I was about to launch into an explanation about Albert's absence when his deep voice issued behind me.

"Hello, everyone," he said, giving me a wry smile. He pulled up a chair next to me and spoke in soft tones. "I decided it would be better to figure all of this out together, rather than alone."

I looked at him in gratitude. "I'm so glad you are here. There's something I want to tell you about, later. About my time..." I paused, looking for the right word, "...my time away."

We were interrupted as several more people entered Maeve's living room. Maeve helped them find places to sit, dragging in folding chairs from the hallway. I recognized Roderick Anderson, a medium I'd met at a recent Sunday service. With him was his wife, Judy, a member of the volunteer board that ran Lily Dale, both of them grey-haired and heavyset, but with the shared gentle energy of a couple who has spent meaningful years working together on matters of the spirit. With them was a third woman I did not know.

Maeve introduced her as Holly Caldwell. She looked to be about forty, her soft auburn curls tinged with a trace of gray, her eyes warm when she turned to me in greeting.

As soon as everyone was seated, Maeve sat in her usual spot in the overstuffed chair and addressed us all, her eyes lingering on Albert for a moment. If she was wondering who inhabited his body, she didn't show it. "I'm delighted to have a special guest with us this evening. Evelyn has driven all the way from Cleveland to join us. I'm excited about what she is going to share, and I've invited several of our friends in the community to sit in on our class. I will let her tell her own story."

Evelyn smiled. She explained that she was a channel, in contact with a group of wise spirits who called themselves The Council of Elders. Prior to connecting with this extraordinary source of spiritual knowledge, she had been a psychologist, spending her days in an office chair listening to people talk about their problems, frustrated by her inability to make progress with many of them. One day, as a woman on her office couch was rehashing her life issues, unable to see that the same challenges occurred in each of her relationships, Evelyn started daydreaming. She was doodling with her pen and making circles at the edges of her notepaper, when she felt a strange sensation in her hand. Curious to see her pen moving, as if on its own, she watched, as the doodles grew larger and more defined.

The client continued a familiar litany of complaints — how people walked all over her, how she just couldn't figure out how to be happy — and she didn't seem to notice odd movement of Evelyn's pen. "Dying," the pen wrote. "She is dying. Tell her she is dying." Evelyn had sat upright in her chair, startled by the words on the page. Her client was dying? She sent a thought out to whomever was writing through her hand. "Dying from what?" Her hand continued its scrawl. "She is dying from life." Evelyn suddenly got an image in her mind of a lamp, with its flame dimming. She then understood that her client was diminishing her own life energy with constant attention on negative things. Her life force was declining to such a degree that it was impacting all the cells in her body. She was killing herself.

Evelyn cleared her throat. "Jenny," she interrupted the woman on the couch, "are you ready to die?"

Jenny stared at Evelyn. "No, of course not. Why?"

Evelyn took a breath. Jenny's issues were clearer to her now than they had ever been. "You are killing yourself," she said, repeating the words on her notepad. Though the diagnosis was not hers, the clarity was. She started hearing other words in her head, and as she pondered them, she realized they made sense. She repeated them to Jenny. "The health of the cells that make up your body are influenced by your emotions. That's been proven by research," she explained. "All your attention right now is on sadness and negativity which causes the cells in your body to slow their vibration. When the vibration in your body slows, the cells don't get as much energy as they need for wellness. You are setting yourself up for illness. So, I'm just asking you, are you ready to die?"

Jenny looked shocked, insisting that, of course she was not ready to die. The question started a whole new line of thinking between the two women about how Jenny's life would look if she decided to live in a manner that sped up the vibration of her body by making choices that brought her joy. Evelyn felt that the energy in the room had shifted by the end of the session. The woman left her office that day with a renewed vigor for remaking her life.

Once Evelyn was alone, she said a silent thank-you to whomever had given her the inspiration on her note pad. She heard clearly, in her mind, the words *"You are welcome."*

Jennifer wasn't the only one changed that day. Evelyn was profoundly moved by the information that came through her hand. She began exploring the possibilities of what had occurred in her office and how her hand had seemed to be taken over by another energy as it wrote the cryptic prescription for her patient. She knew from the beginning that whatever it was, was a gift to her, possibly from her higher self, or a higher being, and she wanted more of that communication. She began studying all kinds of new age therapies, including energy medicines like Reiki and hands-on healing, to learn more about the human energy system without straying too far from the science of her profession. After that, following her intuition, she read a wide variety of books on automatic writing and began meditating each morning with a pen and paper, ready for more communication if it came.

As soon as she opened the metaphysical doorway to the council, they returned to her awareness, and the meditations led to more words of spiritual wisdom scribbled on many more notepads. Eventually, she was writing lengthy messages, worded as if from a wise and compassionate elder. When she shared the messages with a few close friends, they were fascinated. Her friends asked to watch the process and one night, as several sat around her while she meditated, she began speaking in the voice of her communicator. The entity identified itself as a representative of The Council of Elders. A voice that called itself Uriel spoke through her.

As I sat in Maeve's class, watching Evelyn tell her story, I began to feel excited, almost agitated, and very grateful to get more understanding of the channeling process. I looked over at Albert and he appeared to be listening intently, but with a sense of calm disinterest. As a man who had recently channeled my lover who was apparently our soul mate, I was surprised that he didn't appear to feel the same powerful emotions that were occurring within me.

Holly raised her hand, tentatively. Evelyn smiled at her. "You don't have to raise your hand. What would you like to know?"

"How did you know it was information meant to do good, rather than evil?" Holly asked.

Evelyn nodded, contemplating the question. "I have given that a lot of thought," she said. "From the beginning of my work as a counselor, I developed a sense of truth. I could tell which of my patients really wanted help, apart from those who just wanted to complain. I could sense in their stories where the light was and the darkness. So, maybe that's helped me in this," Evelyn said. "I simply knew that this information was good and powerful, because it was helping people."

I understood that. As a fledgling medium, I also knew that the information that came into my head was unquestionably helpful to those that I shared it with. I knew there was goodness in this work, but I had a question, "Evelyn, do you think of this council that you channel as God?"

I saw the light increase within her eyes as if it were a flame. "I believe the divine spirit infuses life into all living things. I believe that spirit is a part of our power as humans and when you hold the intention that your power is to be used for good, then I believe you are doing the work of God."

We sat in silence. I wanted to tell Evelyn about what Albert and Sebastian and I had experienced, but I knew it wasn't just my story. I looked over at Albert to see if he was aware that this was the perfect chance to learn more.

He was way ahead of me. "Evelyn," he said, smiling serenely. "Can the members of the council use your whole body? Can they walk about and do human things. Like... say, dance?"

He looked over at me and I saw the curve of his lips. Dance? Evelyn looked at Albert. I had no idea how she could know, but I felt sure she somehow knew he didn't mean "dance."

"I know there are entities who walk around as they are channeled. It's a powerful experience to watch the entity use the channel's body to rise from a chair and move about. So, yes, I believe that if those entities can walk, they can surely...dance." As she said the word *dance*, her eyes twinkled. Then, she stopped abruptly. "Okay, apparently, the council has something to add. I feel as if they want to come through, so I'm going to say a prayer and surround myself with divine light and we will proceed."

Evelyn closed her eyes and began to breathe deeply. I felt an urge to take Albert's hand, but resisted. It was only a matter of moments before I watched the peacefulness on Evelyn's face begin to change, her mouth moving as if she were about to speak. When she did speak, her voice was deeper, and slightly accented, as if coming from a foreigner.

"Good...evening," she said, looking around the room, smiling broadly. "I am very happy to be here."

Her eyes had taken on a different look. She was squinting, as if getting used to the light. "I am Uriel of the Council of Elders. I want to speak about this place that you call Heaven." Uriel moved his head slowly, his eyes taking in all of us. "Heaven is right here." He looked over at Tracy. She sat up straighter and looked back at him, transfixed. "The people that die, as you say in your language, they are never far from you. Upon death, the spirit which animates the body simply rises from its form like a baby bird, broken free from its shell. Of course, the shell once housed the baby bird as it came forth from its mother. But the bird and the shell separate. The baby bird grows stronger each day and eventually, it begins to flap its wings and fly away," he explained. "The difference is that, with humans, your soul is the baby bird. The shell is your body. Upon death, the soul leaves the body, as a baby bird leaves the shell."

Uriel stopped speaking. Then, perhaps in response to Albert's question about movement, he stood from the chair and began walking around. His steps, taken in Evelyn's body, were measured and regal. "Once out of the shell, the soul vibrates so rapidly that it can fly away to new adventures, but some souls stay near their shells for a long time."

We were transfixed as Uriel returned to his chair, sat down with his back erect, and continued. "So, this newly freed soul attempts to stay, trying to connect with its loved ones, who are often oblivious from their grief. The soul, unencumbered by the density of the human body is vibrating so quickly that, like the spinning blades of a fan, it cannot be seen with the human eye. So often, when those left behind offer no response, the adventures presented by this new freedom are made clearer." Uriel, through Evelyn's eyes, scanned our faces to see who understood his words. He stopped and looked at me, smiled again and said, "You may breathe now."

I laughed lightly as I exhaled. He continued without missing a beat. "The soul begins to explore the promises within this new environment, often reveling in an extraordinary feeling of youthfulness and energy, in some case, pain-free for the first time in a long while." He described the soul's newly discovered mobility as akin to our astronauts in space, and asked us to imagine how easily they fly through the air in a gravity-free environment. "That's how your soul feels outside of your body."

He walked over to a little electric fan that Maeve kept on her desk, and flipped the switch to the "on" position. The fan demonstrated his explanation perfectly, and as it began to spin, we watched its petals disappear in a whir of movement. "If you are able to speed your vibration through meditation, or prayer, or by participating in something that brings you joy, like dancing or singing, you can sometimes see us, or feel us about. And if we work hard, we can slow our vibration to be with you in physical form," he added. "That is exactly what I am doing right now, so I can sit among you," he smiled, raising his arms out, palms up, in a gesture of a magician revealing a trick.

Uriel described the place a newly freed soul goes as simply another dimension of existence, where one's energy can be used to easily create matter such as gardens, or homes, or places to gather. "As you know, there are many gifts to being a human," he said. "The benefits, certainly, are human sensations and human connection. That is why we come back to form, because the ability to taste and to touch and to satisfy the needs of the body is sometimes so magnificent." Long before we were finished asking questions, Uriel began to take his leave. "There is just one more thing I have to say before I depart this evening." He looked directly at Albert and then at me. "As you learn the abilities that come with raising your vibration, some get a little confused about the ultimate goal of living in physical form," he said. His dark eyes scanned my face, and then moved to Albert's. " You will all be here where I am, soon enough," he said. "If you get too caught up with those of us who are here in my dimension, you will miss out on your existence. The fruits of your time here will be wasted, despite all the effort you exerted to come here." He walked over to the stool and sat down, once again surveying those in the room. His eyes stopped for a moment on each face to give a nod of recognition. "I bid you a pleasant good night. We are always at your service."

And then, Uriel was gone. The room seemed to have less energy in it as we looked at each other, a little stunned. Even in Lily Dale, where people regularly communed with spirits, such things did not happen every day. I felt like I was wading through a river of miracles. We all stared at Evelyn as she sat there in the middle of the room, perched on a stool with her eyes shut. Slowly, she came back to us, and when her eyelids opened, she blinked against the soft lights. "So," Evelyn smiled, "you've met Uriel and the council."

We nodded.

"Questions?" she asked. We all started talking at once.

Tracy wanted to know if anyone could contact the council on his or her own. Evelyn told her that each of us has our advisors in spirit. Accessing them is the challenge, she said, for it requires a peaceful, happy soul, and no expectation of outcome.

Albert spoke next. "Can they come and go at will?"

Evelyn shook her head emphatically. "Absolutely not. The channel must be open and willing to encounter the guides."

Guides. I was a little jealous of Evelyn's ease with the term. I wanted guides. Sebastian didn't count as a guide exactly, although he certainly had provided me with some guidance in our short time together, particularly during our little excursion into the afterlife. He was more like the return of something I'd lost, but didn't know I was missing. I looked over at Albert.

He was watching Evelyn as she talked. Her face was animated, and her eyes were filled with light. Albert seemed mesmerized by her.

Earlier in the day, when Albert had come back to his body during our lovemaking, I had imagined that he was so affronted by the situation, I might never see Sebastian again in Albert's form. But watching Albert's face as he listened to Evelyn, as we heard about how much her work helped others to understand that there was more life after this one, I could tell something was changing inside of him. Then, he looked in my direction and our eyes caught, and I understood. Peering out from Albert's spectacles, once more, was the energetic, playful, and adoring eyes of my lovely Sebastian.

21

As soon as I sensed Sebastian, the energy in the room changed. I couldn't take my eyes off him. Each time he inhabited Albert's body, I was more captivated by the change that occurred in the energy within the professor's form. His nearness had the effect of an energetic youth serum. I felt beautiful and eternal, my own energy amplified as if I could send sparks flying forth from my fingertips.

"There's more to do," he whispered, leaning so close to me I could feel his breath on my ear.

"What do you mean?" I whispered back, inhaling the musky scent of Albert's neck, which now smelled exactly like Sebastian.

I stayed in that position one moment too long and Maeve seemed to notice. Then Evelyn turned to look at us. When she stopped talking, everyone else looked our way.

"There is someone else here with us," Evelyn said, looking at Sebastian.

"You've come to meet with the council, then?" she asked.

He smiled, and took my hand. "Well, actually..." he said, "I've already met with them. They encouraged me to return, as I have this...one more thing," he said, looking at me. "Rebecca has been helping me make things right with my daughter and my granddaughter, but there's one more thing I need to do."

One more thing? I straightened in my chair. We had just set everything in order over at Beth and Anne's. Beth was safe. What else was there to do? I stared at Sebastian, remembering how it felt to kiss that jaw with its scratchy shadow of a beard. A squeeze of Sebastian's hand pulled me out of my reverie.

Maeve spoke my thoughts. "And Albert, has he given you permission to use his form?"

Sebastian shrugged charmingly. "Well, it appears that Albert and I are in this together. It seems that we three," and he turned to include me in his words, "we have this agreement to...help each other." Sebastian explained to us that his ex-wife, Victoria, was dying. He hadn't seen her in years; she hadn't wanted to see him. But she had heard from Anne and Beth about his reappearance and while she didn't quite believe them, she was desperately afraid to die. He wanted to prove to her that it was truly he who had managed to return to help their granddaughter. It was the least he could do, he said, for this woman whose heart he'd broken long ago. He wanted to beg her forgiveness and relieve her fears about what was coming next.

"I was a very bad husband," he confessed to the group, "and I need to make it up to her. When it's time, I plan to accompany her out of this life into the next, but I'd like to talk with her first, to calm her fears. After that, I don't expect to be returning here in physical form until Rebecca makes her transition. Then I'll be coming for her, as well."

My heart fell. I was already sad to hear that Anne's mother would soon die. I couldn't bear to be reminded that once Sebastian left me, I wouldn't be seeing him again for a very long time.

As if he could hear my thoughts, he raised my hand to his lips and kissed my knuckles gently. I wondered if those in the room, so much more sensitive than most to human energy, could see the sparks that flew off my body and merged with his, causing a jolt I felt in the pit of my stomach, like a flash of tiny fireworks.

Evelyn didn't seem to notice, still processing Sebastian's words about his wife. "How can we help," she asked.

"I need to speak to Albert," he said. "Can you make that happen?"

Evelyn nodded. "I'll see." She closed her eyes once more and we all watched expectantly as she went into a trance.

Uriel returned, blinking in awareness. "I understand you need my assistance," he intoned. "I will seek the entity known as Albert." We watched as Evelyn's face went blank, and after several minutes, it seemed like nothing would occur.

Then I heard Albert's baritone. "Sebastian," he said evenly, "you did not ask permission and that's wrong. If I weren't going to be hitting my own self, I'd punch you in the nose."

Sebastian smiled sheepishly. "Albert, hello," he said in relief. "I am so glad we could make this work."

"Make this work?" Albert sputtered through Evelyn. "How is this working? You've co-opted my body, and now you're behaving as if Rebecca is all yours when in fact, we've seen that we three are in this together. If you're going to disappear and I'm going to stick around here without Julia, then I'm going to need Rebecca more than you do. So back off; you cannot take her with you!"

I raised my eyebrows in alarm. "Albert," I said, trying to reason with him like I might with one of my grade-schoolers, "I'm not going with him..." I didn't finish. I knew that Albert and I were forming an unusual bond. I realized that if Sebastian was going to leave me and I couldn't go with him, then I really wanted Albert to stay in my life.

In Evelyn's body, Albert rubbed his head and for a moment I could see he was feeling Evelyn's shorn scalp. Then he looked down at Evelyn's thin, feminine hands and manicured nails. He seemed to calm a bit and smiled ruefully. "Okay, this is a change. It appears I'm a woman," he said. "I can feel her peaceful nature."

Sebastian cut in with a chuckle. "But only for a few moments, old friend. I'm going to guess it's superior to being in your body, which I can see hasn't done a full set of pushups since high school."

Albert's brow shot up. "You should speak more kindly of my body, considering you keep borrowing it from me."

The others chuckled at the exchange.

"Look, Albert," Sebastian pleaded, "I need to do this. At some point in our futures you'll be doing the same thing for me, but right now I need your body. I need Rebecca. I don't have much time and I promise, it will all work out in the end."

Albert narrowed Evelyn's green eyes, and surveyed Sebastian staring back at him through his own brown eyes. "You know I will allow it, but if I ever need help from you in the future, I expect you will be available to me, no matter where you are," Albert responded.

Sebastian smiled. "Anything, anywhere, my friend. I'll be there for you."

Albert did not respond. We were all staring at Evelyn as she sat on the stool in the middle of the room, her back ramrod straight, eyes closed. We could see that Albert was no longer in use of her body. Her feminine face softened, looking serene. Her eyelids fluttered open, and she surveyed us before inhaling deeply. Her body seemed to relax. "Well, did that help?" She looked about the room, hopeful.

Sebastian nodded at her, gratefully. "I have his blessing to use this body for just a bit longer," he told her. "I'm just wondering if you have any idea how long these experiences can last before depleting the host?"

Evelyn was still. "In my experience these things last exactly as long as they need to."

We left Maeve's house shortly after that, as Sebastian could feel Albert's body starting to tire. "I don't want to overwork the old boy," he whispered, when we stood to leave and I gathered my things.

As we walked onto the darkened streets of Lily Dale, Sebastian and I talked softly so as not to disturb the peace of the community in the late evening. Off in the distance I heard several geese calling to each other on the lake. Sebastian reached for my hand and I gave it willingly. We walked for a time in silence, until I remembered the experience we'd shared in meditation.

"Sebastian, when we were...out there," I said, pointing upwards, "I learned we were together in many lives."

He nodded. "Yes."

"You and Albert and me," I said.

He walked beside me in silence.

"So, why do I feel so completely connected to you, and not so much to him?" I asked.

We stopped on the darkened path and faced each other. I looked up into Albert's face and saw no trace of the professor. Just the probing eyes of Sebastian, dark and loving and wise. The nearness of his body to mine raised a response in my heart that belonged to Sebastian alone. There was no trace of confusion as to who stood before me.

"My good luck?" he asked in bemused reply.

We embraced, and I put my head on Sebastian's chest, listening to Albert's heart thumping in response "I want you to stay," I whispered.

Such love was etched across his face that I nearly stopped breathing in awe of it. Then, he kissed my forehead. "Rebecca. You know I can't."

We continued our walk through the darkness. With each step I was closer to losing Sebastian. Unless...

As we entered my little apartment and fell upon my bed in an embrace once more, I couldn't get the thought out of my head. It kept returning louder and louder. When he leaves, I am going with him. There was no lovemaking that night, but lying in my bed in Sebastian's arms, I did not miss it. Albert's body needed rest, as did mine. Just being next to Sebastian's spirit, feeling our energies blend together, was a form of making love. It was as if he were a river and I was an inlet, and the movement of his spirit swirled within mine in constant flow, awash in a peacefulness that felt like the highest possible union between two beings. With Sebastian beside me, I was completely and finally whole. I didn't sleep much that night. All I could think about was the small amount of time I had left with him. I tried not to see it as his death, for he had already died. By virtue of his sleeping soundly next to me, it was clear that death was not permanent. But now that I had experienced his presence, I never wanted him to leave.

Despite the discomfort of my musings, when the morning came I felt rested and invigorated, possibly due to the infusion of Sebastian's spirit into my own, renewing me in the blending of our energies. His eyes flew open at around seven a.m. He pulled me close. I inhaled his scent, musky and masculine, trying to remember exactly how he smelled so I would never forget it. He rose quickly and began to dress in Albert's trousers and cotton shirt. Every time I looked at him, it was as if I was seeing him for the first time. I couldn't believe how the beauty that emanated from his spirit transformed Albert's physical being. It was still amazing to me that, despite his being in Albert's body, which was thicker and less graceful than his own former physique, his appearance to me was that of the Sebastian as I had first seen him, much younger than Albert and more elegant in in structure, each muscle firm and defined where Albert, while though trim and fit, was a bit puffier and pale. I wasn't sure how that worked, but I wasn't interested in figuring it all out just then. I hoped I'd have some time to do that later.

Time. I closed my eyes, and I wondered how much time we had. "Sebastian, how are we going to do this?"

I asked as I watched him dress. He reached a hand out and I gave him mine. One gentle pull and I was on my feet.

His eyes looked concerned. "I'm not sure." His arms wrapped around me and he pressed his body against mine. We stood like that for a moment and then he cleared his throat and spoke. "Let's go to Victoria and we'll try and figure it out from there."

We got in my car and, following Sebastian's directions, I was able to easily find Victoria's apartment building. I had to resist driving like a madwoman. Sebastian was certain Victoria was in a struggle for her life. I parked at the curb in front of her first floor apartment. We walked quickly to her doorway and rang the bell. A handsome elderly woman answered the door and when I saw her, I thought that Sebastian had somehow been mistaken. She certainly didn't look unwell. Victoria was a lovely woman of average build, impeccably dressed, wearing a white cardigan over a navy sheath, her silver hair pulled into a tight chignon. She raised her eyebrows when she saw us, two strangers standing in her doorway.

Sebastian was silent. I decided to introduce myself. "Hello Victoria. My name is Rebecca St. Claire," I told her. "I am the medium from Lily Dale who connected your daughter and granddaughter to Sebastian. I know they've told you about that. I was wondering if we could come in for a few minutes."

Victoria looked at me quizzically. "Miss St. Claire, I appreciate what you did for Beth, but I have a bridge game in a half hour."

"Victoria." Sebastian cleared his throat. "My name is Albert Cummings. I am a medium like Miss St. Claire. We study together..."

I watched, fascinated, as Sebastian tried to channel a little bit of Albert. He shifted uncomfortably on the cement steps leading up to Victoria's door and tugged at the hem of his shirt for good measure, in an Albert-like manner. "I have been channeling your ex-husband, Sebastian, and it has been a very...interesting experience," he told her. "He's insistent about passing along some messages to you. "

She squinted at my companion, reassessing him, her brows lifting as she realized he was the man who assisted her granddaughter, claiming to somehow be connected to her dead ex-husband. "Yes," Anne told me about you..." Her eyes were still on Sebastian and she pursed her lips as she considered our request.

"All right, come in, but I don't have much time. Let me just make a quick phone call to let them know I might be late."

She walked out of the room and we heard her speaking quietly on a phone. I took the time to look around. Victoria's apartment was a decorated in serene, welcoming shades of blue and white, embellished by a vase of beautiful blue and yellow tulips on the coffee table.

We stood uncomfortably near her door while we waited. I looked over at Sebastian and whispered, "Albert? Now, you're Albert?"

He shrugged. "You have to work with what you've got. What would you have me do?"

"I never lie," I whispered sharply.

He nodded solemnly and the corner of his lip turned up as he suppressed a grin. "And that is why you are such a good woman. Me, I'm still working on my redemption."

"Well, this is going to set you back," I said.

"We shall see," he whispered, as Victoria walked into the room.

"Would you like a cup of coffee?" she asked us, clearly not in the mood to play hostess.

We declined the coffee and she motioned to the couch and chairs in the living room. "Well then, have a seat. Tell me what you've come to say."

Sebastian and I sat down next to each other on the sofa. Victoria sat at the edge of a cushioned chair.

"Your ex-husband keeps showing up in my head," Sebastian began. "He seems concerned about you."

She had been staring at her tightly clasped hands. She raised her eyes and looked at Sebastian intently, one perfectly shaped eyebrow raised in question. "Don't you think it's a little late for him to be concerned about me?"

"Mrs. Morgan, things happen to us when we die. We get...understanding about the impact our lives have had on other people. He wants you to know that from where he is, he realizes how hard you worked to raise Anne and what a good woman you are. He's deeply sorry for how he treated you and wants to make it up to you."

Victoria's eyes got a little teary. Mine did too, as I watched this man try to work his way back in to his ex-wife's heart.

She bit her lip, thinking. "Mr. Cummings, I'm not a vengeful woman. I have learned that you can't carry that kind of anger around. It isn't good for you."

Sebastian stood and walked over to Victoria. He knelt before her and took both her hands. "Victoria, it's back. The leukemia has returned. Sebastian wanted me to tell you that it is not yet your time. The new treatments you are considering will give you many more months if you want them, with less difficulty than the last time. He just thought you might like to know that."

Victoria sighed again, this time more deeply. Her pretenses dropped. "I know it's back. I had a dream the other night about weeds in my garden. I had pulled them all out, but they returned with a vengeance." She shook her head. "Funny, because in that dream, the vegetables were beautiful. I couldn't believe the way they grew anyway; the tomatoes were about as big as my head. There was zucchini everywhere, bushels and bushels." She rubbed her forehead, and stood up. "Look, I've got to go. Tell Sebastian 'thank you,' and..." she looked right into Sebastian's eyes and put her hand on his face. I couldn't tell if she knew that she was speaking to her ex-husband, but her words were soft as she patted his cheek, "tell him that I forgave him a long time ago."

I saw pain in Sebastian's eyes. "Thank you, Victoria. He said to tell you that when you cross, he doesn't want you to be afraid. He will be there if you wish, to take your hand and guide your way" Sebastian told her. "All you have to do is ask."

She stared into his eyes for a moment. "That's an interesting offer. I will consider it." Her brow furrowed, she appeared to want to say something more, but then waved a hand toward the door "I really have to go," she said.

She looked at me and blinked, as if she'd forgotten I was there. She paused for a moment, as if finally seeing me. "Thank you for helping my girls," she said softly.

"It's my honor to help in any way that I can," I replied. As tears gathered in her eyes, she shut the door firmly.

I waited until we were near the car before I spoke. "So, that went well," I said, trying to infuse a little lightness into the deeply personal moment I had just witnessed. "Except for the lying part."

He sighed. "She didn't buy it for a minute. She's a pretty smart cookie."

I stopped on the sidewalk. "She knew?"

"She knew."

On the ride home, he was visibly subdued. I could feel a decline in his energy, and when he turned to say something to me as I drove, his words came out slowly.

"I can feel this body tiring," he said. "I'm having trouble moving it."

I had wondered when that was going to happen. I still didn't understand how a spirit was able to inhabit a human body for long periods of time, but from what I had seen in my trip to the afterlife, Sebastian and Albert were very connected. Perhaps that's why they were able to sustain the channel. It was clear we didn't have much time left.

"Sebastian, you're going to have to leave me soon."

"I know," he replied. He moved his hand over to the edge of his seat, and I took my right hand off the wheel and placed it atop his. "It's going to be a while before I can return to you," he said, putting words to a sadness that was growing within me.

"I know."

"This thing that we have," he continued slowly, "what we're doing...life is not meant to be like this."

A tear slipped down my cheek and I wiped it away with the back of my hand.

"From my perspective, as a dead man..." He paused to watch for my smile at his words, but I kept my eyes on the road ahead as I tried to repress my alarm. "...I am aware that we will be together in a very short time. But I know that for you, there will be many long years before we can hold each other again."

I gripped the wheel tighter. Sebastian was saying goodbye to me. "Not yet," I whispered. "I'm not ready."

Sebastian's voice sounded tired, and his eyes started to close.

"Sebastian, wait!" I shouted, but I could see him slipping away.

"There are so many things I want to learn..." he mumbled.

With a yank of the steering wheel, I pulled over to the side of the road. With shaking hands and jumped out of the car, tearing around to the other side of the vehicle and flinging open the passenger door. "Sebastian," I pleaded. "Don't leave me yet."

I put my hands on each side of his face and watched as Sebastian receded from Albert's body until his eyes went vacant and the lids closed. I stood next to him, leaning into my car, my hands still on his face, tears streaming down my cheeks as Sebastian's features softened and reshaped into Albert's face.

I stood there for a few moments, waiting for Albert. His eyes remained closed and his breathing was shallow. After a while, I put my head to his chest. I could barely feel his heartbeat. It appeared that once again, Sebastian was gone and Albert was missing. But, this time, I was far more frightened.

Panicked, I flew around to the driver's side, got in and buckled my seatbelt. I pulled my car back out on the road, talking to Albert the whole time. "Come on, Albert, come back to me," I said loudly, "it's time to come back into your body." I kept talking to him as I drove, but Albert's body was unresponsive. He looked pale, and was barely breathing. I worried the channeling experience had been too much for him.

"I'm so sorry, Albert." He did not respond. I began to feel frantic. I desperately wanted Albert to return to his body. If we had somehow hurt him, I would never be able to forgive myself. He was the professor again, his thinning hair patted down over the bald spots, his cheeks flaccid. Even the clothes he wore seemed more scrunched and unfashionable. There wasn't a trace of Sebastian left. But there didn't seem to be much of Albert left, either. I pushed my foot down on the gas pedal and sped to Lily Dale. I needed Maeve's help once again. And I needed it quickly.

22

I honked the horn as I pulled up in front of Maeve's house, hoping she wasn't in the middle of a reading. I felt a rush of relief when she pushed the curtain aside and peered out the window. Maeve would know what to do. I waved at her and in a moment she came out and hurried to my driver's side window. "What's the matter?" she asked.

"We need your help. Again," I said. "Sebastian has left, possibly for good, and I can't get Albert to come back to his body."

Maeve peered past me to get a look at Albert in my passenger's seat. He was still out cold. "Oh, my," she said. "We need to get him inside."

She went around to the passenger door and opened it. I got out of the car and ran to help her. We managed to pull Albert onto his feet next to the curb but he was dead weight and I knew we couldn't move him inside ourselves.

"Albert," I said, patting his cheeks softly. "You've got to wake up."

I breathed a sigh of relief when he began to rouse. He was like a man who'd been sucker-punched, half-conscious, head hanging, but at least he was able to help us get him inside. He hung onto our shoulders as we walked him into the house and laid him on the couch in the living room. Then he was out cold once more. I put my hand on Albert's heart to make sure it was still beating and was relieved to feel a strong, rhythmic thump. Despite that, I was worried, and looked at Maeve in desperation. "What can we do?"

My teacher and mentor, ever the calm, wise woman, patted her hair back into place. "Let's see if we can tap into some guidance," she replied.

I nodded. Of course, when in doubt, check the divine GPS. Once again we both pulled up chairs next to Albert. I watched as Maeve sat, closed her eyes and began to breathe in deep, even breaths. I did the same, but struggled to release the emotional events of the day.

Maeve opened her eyes. The information had come quickly. "Albert is a diabetic. I'm being told he needs his medication, *now*," she said, standing up from her chair. "His low blood sugar, coupled with the exertion of the channeling had slowed his system to nearly a complete stop. Do you know where he lives?"

I shook my head to tell her no, and my face flushed. Considering how intimate I'd been with Albert over the last few days, it was odd that I had no idea where he lived. I had only been interested in Sebastian and where he lived. I felt guilty for being so single-minded when Albert had been so kind, and made a mental note to try to make it up to him when he came back from...wherever he was. We searched his pockets and found his wallet and house key. His address was on his driver's license. I grabbed his keys and my own and ran from the house. Once I punched his address into my car's GPS, I realized I was only about a few miles away from where he lived outside of Lily Dale.

I pulled up into the driveway of his home, a small, blue ranch in a community of tidy farm homes and trim, green pastures, and jumped from my car. I was fairly certain he lived alone, but before I put the key in the door I knocked, just to make sure. When I heard no reply, I twisted the key and opened the door. Albert's place was as I expected it to be. Leather furniture, dark wood, books placed meticulously on shelves that rose to the ceiling in both the living room and an adjacent study that I could see through an open door. A desk had orderly stacks of paper upon it and a set of pens waited nearby, as if he planned to sit and write sometime soon. I went to the back of the house to his bedroom and bathroom, where I hoped I might find his medication. I stood in front of a shelf in the bathroom where, among several small medicine bottles, I found a long plastic pill case, marked with the days of the week. I could see that he had not taken his pills in two days.

I was heading out the door when something caught my eye across the kitchen. Off to one side was a small room filled with paintings and paint supplies, brushes and paper. On the floor, propped against the walls, were dozens of watercolor portraits and landscapes. Many were of a beautiful, blonde woman, her blue eyes crinkled in laughter, or looking out at the painter with a loving expression. Julia. I was touched by how tenderly she was depicted by her husband.

I noticed a painting sitting on the easel in the middle of the room, obviously a work in progress. I stopped in my tracks and stared. It was a painting of me, standing at the edge of the lake, looking out at the water, my face lit with recognition for someone just outside of the picture. Albert had painted my hair the way I wore it before I'd met him, long and dark, blowing loose off my shoulders. As Albert depicted me, I was gorgeous, not in a youthful, hard-bodied kind of way, but rather as a woman at the edge of her mid-life, yet full of vitality, and radiating passion for something, or someone. I only allowed myself a few seconds to take in the unfinished painting, but I longed to stand there and notice every detail. Later, I would ask Albert about it. Right then, I had to bring him his medication.

It didn't take long to get back to Maeve's home. Together, she and I got Albert to swallow his medication and sip some orange juice to help balance his sugar. He muttered his thanks and then fell back to sleep on the couch. While we waited for his body to absorb the pills, I told Maeve about the picture. Then I filled her in on the flashbacks I'd seen of Sebastian and Albert and me being together in many lives, somehow connected through the centuries. It struck me as odd that in this lifetime, Albert's presence prior to these last few days had not alerted me in any way to our mystical connection. To me, he was just a fellow student in my mediumship class who was quiet and seemed pleasant enough. But he hadn't triggered an emotional response in me as Sebastian had, in a manner that sent energy swirling through my body, raised the little hairs on my arms, and made me feel utterly alive.

Had I not had the experiences with Sebastian and Albert, I would have never known Albert and I were connected in any special way. I wouldn't have remembered him as a serious young boy, eager to learn the ways of the world through his books and research. I suddenly understood how hard it must have been for him to look beyond his disciplined studies to experience such an unconventional aspect of life. I had been so fixated on Sebastian, that Albert had become a means to an end, a way to connect with Sebastian. While I knew he was giving us a great gift, I never fully appreciated him. Now, perhaps because I had learned in the afterlife that we were connected through time, or perhaps because I stumbled upon his beautiful depiction of me, I saw Albert in a whole new light.

My eyes wandered across his sleeping face. Staring at the contours of his cheeks and his high forehead, I saw the gentle countenance of a man who had never raised a hand to anyone, who always spoke thoughtfully and considered things deeply. This was a man whose heart was broken by the death of his beloved wife, Julia and instead of retreating into the darkness of grief, he was spending his retirement years trying to understand where she had gone. He loaned us his body, knowing I would be with Sebastian and despite the possibility that he, Albert, might have some feelings for me. He was such a kind man, but in these last few days, had I been a kind woman?

I had gotten a little off-track when I met Sebastian. I was drawn into the excitement of connecting to a spirit in such a provable, physical way and Sebastian had been so wondrous and compelling. He was precious to me, a part of my own soul. But the man right in front of me, who was still a living, breathing human, was also somehow a part of my soul and had apparently understood our relationship long before I had. Missing from all of our experiences was my gratitude to Albert for the miraculous connection to the divine that shattered all my notions about why we are alive on this planet. My brush with divine love gave me clear understanding that nothing happens by chance. We are all here by our own intention, deliberately testing our mettle through challenges and gifts unavailable to us in a perfect Heaven. These were revelations unlike any I'd experienced in my long academic quest for knowledge. They were simple spiritual truths that some people say aloud every day, but that most don't truly grasp.

I made a vow to myself. For the rest of my life, I would aspire to help others become aware of the human connection to spirit. I now knew that without that awareness, no matter how many gifts we received in our lives, there would always be a place within that felt disconnected and lonely. Inside my head, I saw my beautiful mother and my tiny grandmother, standing together. They were clearly delighted I was stepping into the legacy of hope and faith that they'd left for me. I felt tears fill my eyes at seeing them together. They were proud of me, but how did I feel about myself? I had started the summer at Lily Dale as a broken woman, just trying to return to the peace and pleasures of my childhood. Had I lost what remained of myself in Sebastian? Or, had I found myself and so much more?

I looked over at Albert and saw his eyelids fluttering. "Albert," I whispered. "Are you there?" He opened his eyes and stared at the ceiling for a few seconds. Then he turned his head, and our eyes locked. In his penetrating gaze, I could see enough to understand that something had changed in our relationship. He knew it, too.

"Well, I guess I am," he said in response to my question, offering a languid half-smile. "That was pretty amazing."

"Where were you?" I asked, keeping my voice soft so as not to disturb the gentle energy that was swirling between us.

"I was with Julia, again. We were in some sort of library, going through books, and sharing bits of our life together, places we had been and, my God, she looked so lovely. Like an angel, with this magnificent light surrounding her..." A tear dripped from the corner of his eye. "She said we were not going to be together again for what might seem a very long while. She said there are many things I need to do in this life and that I can't do them if I'm bound to her. When I was with her, I understood completely and was eager to return," he said, "but now that I'm here, I'm afraid to let go. I'm afraid I'll forget her." He shut his eyes, as if to block the sight of me.

I knew, sitting there at Albert's side, my heart aching for us both, that he and I had some things to do together in this life before we joined our loved ones on the other side. And then, something shifted within my broken heart. My love for Sebastian, which felt eternal, moved gently aside and made room for Albert.

"Albert, I know just how you feel," I told him. "I'm not going to see Sebastian for a while. He told me so before he left. But I have a feeling that Julia is right. You and I still have some work to do in this life."

Our conversation was interrupted by Maeve, who entered the room with a tray holding a teapot and several cups, her solution for any ailment. "Ah, good. You're back," she told Albert, as she set the tray down on the table in front of the couch. "They told me it would only be a matter of time," she added, a quick glance of her eyes skyward to indicate she was speaking of her guides. She observed him for a moment. "You look like you came through it okay," she smiled.

Albert smiled weakly. "Yes, I'm back."

"I'm so happy for you," she said, pulling a straight-backed chair closer to the couch. She put a hand on Albert's shoulder. "Once you're feeling up to it, I'm hoping we can work on strengthening your connection with the other side. We've somehow made a deeper connection than anyone's been able to before...and I would like to help you explore that connection."

She looked at me. "It could bring comfort to a lot of people."

I nodded. I had thought Sebastian was my destiny. But as I sat next to Albert, I knew that destiny was more bountiful than that as we worked together to fortify the connection between this life and the next. I could not wait to begin. But first, there were some things we needed to discuss.

"I stopped at your house to get your medication," I said to him. He nodded, and then his eyes widened.

"You did?"

"Yes, I did," I confessed.

"And ... you saw my house," he continued warily.

"Yes, I did," I repeated.

"So, you probably saw ... "

I nodded. "It was breathtaking."

Our eyes caught, and he was quiet for a few moments before he said quietly, "When I began to paint you, I didn't understand why. We were just classmates, but there was something about you, something I couldn't quite put my finger on, that made me feel drawn to you."

I was still as a stone, unable to believe what I was hearing. He reached for my hand. When our fingers touched, I felt a familiar pulse of energy, but this was far gentler than the little explosions that occurred when I touched Sebastian.

"I was feeling terribly guilty about that, because of my love for Julia. I was trying to capture your essence on my canvas so I could understand what was drawing me to you. And then Sebastian came along and well, you know the rest."

He told me that in the time he spent with Julia's spirit, they had discussed Sebastian and me, and she had told Albert of her love for each of us. She said that while she had never shared lives with us before, she was now part of the evolution of our soul group, and that we would continue to come back together in new lifetimes, taking different roles in an effort to experience all aspects of the possibilities of human growth. Albert and I talked for much of the afternoon, with Maeve administering tea and wisdom when needed. We talked about the afterlife experiences we had shared and when we had a question, Maeve would ask her guides and they would deliver information. Life, as we came to agree that afternoon, was a lot simpler than it seemed. The one abiding truth is that when we take human form, we are spiritual energy animating bodies made from much slower-moving energy. An important part of the experience is to forget we are spirits, but there is joy to be found in remembering.

Later that afternoon, Albert regained his strength and got up from the couch, a bit shaky, but ready to return home. Maeve and I helped him to my car and we tucked him into the passenger's seat before I got into the driver's side. She waved us off as I drove down the road. All I could think about was our future together, Albert's and mine, not as lovers so much, although I already knew that I loved him. More importantly, I considered what we would teach others. Together, we would share our evidence of life after death, and the wisdom we'd gleaned from the amazing time we'd spent in the afterlife. There was so much more to learn, and now I had a partner to learn with.

I stopped in front of his house. He reached for the doorknob. "Are you okay getting in?" I asked.

He nodded. "I'm pretty tired," he said. "I just want to spend some time alone not thinking about anything. My brain needs a rest."

I understood exactly how he felt. "I'll see you tomorrow," I told him before driving off. I, too, needed some time alone. I was already missing Sebastian, but while the space he'd just vacated could never be filled by anyone, I knew that Albert was going to be at my side for the remainder of my life. And my heart was filled with hope.

23

It's funny that, when I had finally made my peace with death, I was released from its grip. About a week after Sebastian left me, I went to my doctor for a six-month follow-up to determine the success of my radiation and chemotherapy. She did several tests, including a sonogram, and when she came back into the exam room with the results, I already knew what she was going to say.

"It's good news." She smiled, settling herself on a stool near the exam table where I waited in my pink paper gown.

I nodded, surprisingly unaffected. After Sebastian and I had merged, I knew a few things for certain: If I remained in my body, I had a lot of wonderful work to do with Albert, but if I left my body? I would race right into Sebastian's arms. So, even if my doctor had delivered grim results, it was all good.

I didn't hear from Albert the next day, or the following day. It didn't matter; my insight about our eternal connection made me feel like he was never far from me. I used the free time to catch up on my reading and continued to learn more about the kaleidoscope my world had become. I gathered a variety of books on mediumship from the Lily Dale library, but as I flipped through them, none seemed to help me to understand my experience with Sebastian and Albert, or with Beth and Anne for that matter. The physicality of the channeling — the coming to life of a dead person using the body of another — was mentioned occasionally, but more often while the channel was sitting quietly in the midst of listeners. Entities could speak through channels for hours on end, and on occasion get up from their chairs and walk about. Seth, channeled by Jane Roberts, occasionally enjoyed a cigarette when she channeled him for her husband and their friends. Esther Hicks channeled Abraham in large halls filled with people, taking breaks only for "a brief pause for refreshment," when called for by Abraham.

I couldn't find any references to experiences where the entity did more physical things with the borrowed body, like get into a fistfight, or make love with a beloved. Was this a newer and deeper connection between the living and the dead? Or was this just an anomaly, made possible by the connection between the souls of those involved and Sebastian's desperation to help his daughter and granddaughter?

Several days passed, and I was anxious to see Albert that evening in Maeve's class, but I didn't feel a sense of urgency; I was calm and peaceful, reading a book by a woman who'd written about the contact she'd made with her dead son through a medium. Between the woman, the medium, and the son's spirit, they had started a blog to dispense thoughts and information from the afterlife. The medium channeled the spirit of the boy and talked for him. As far as I could tell, she hadn't allowed him to use her body. The more I read, the more I was coming to understand that far more people were experiencing mystical occurrences than I had ever dreamed and they all offered the same basic messages, every last one of them. Don't sweat the small stuff *or* the large stuff. Everything is as it should be and it is always, only about love.

I was so engaged in my book, the knock at the door made me jump. I got up from the rocker and stepped to the porch railing to get a better view of the door to my apartment. It was Albert. I was so happy to see him; I smiled and waved, feeling a little like Juliet as I leaned over the railing. "Hello!"

He looked up with worried eyes. The thinning strands of his hair were combed meticulously back off his forehead, and he wore a simple brown cotton summer jacket and beige khakis. He looked handsome in his distinguished way and squinted through his wire-rimmed glasses. "I'm glad you're home. May I come in?"

"Of course," I called back. "The door is open. Come on up."

As I walked into the house from the porch, I could hear his measured steps on the creaky wooden stairs. By the time he arrived at my door, I had already checked my hair and straightened my purple tunic top over my black yoga pants. My eyes, looking back at me from the mirror, were peaceful. When I saw him push open the door, I felt a rush of anticipation. Impossible things had been happening so often between us, I felt like miracles were becoming second nature to our relationship. But as he walked closer to me, I could see he was upset.

"He's back," Albert said abruptly. "He won't go away."

I bit my lip. I was stunned by the news, but I knew just whom he meant, and my heart thumped. "Who? Sebastian?"

He nodded affirmatively, breathing hard from exasperation combined with the walk up my stairs. "He won't stay out of my head."

"Well, what does he want?" I asked. I felt like a teen-aged girl who had just heard that her boyfriend was back in town. Sebastian had told me he wouldn't be seeing me again for a long while. I had been prepared for that, but not for this.

"What do you think he wants?" he asked ruefully. "He wants you." He said it in the tone of one of my second graders. I had to hide a smile.

I felt such love for Albert just then, but it was soft, consoling love. I wanted to give him a warm hug. Thinking about whether Sebastian was nearby, I knew the difference between my feelings for the two. I was human after all, and Sebastian and I had made a physical and spiritual connection that took me places I had never been before...places I wasn't sure any woman had ever been before. But after a few seconds, I was fairly certain Albert was wrong. I couldn't feel Sebastian, and I couldn't see his energy, even the smallest spark of light, anywhere around us.

"Albert, how do you know it's Sebastian?"

"How do I know it's him?" I could see the question caught him unaware. "Because you are all I can think about," he admitted in frustration. He described how he had been doing handiwork around his house for the past two days, busy work really, making repairs, fixing a broken window in the library, replacing a kitchen faucet, pulling weeds from the garden. "I was just trying to get everything out of my mind so I could think clearly about what has been happening to all of us, but all I could think about was you. The image I couldn't get out of my head was when I came back into my body and found myself in the middle of making love to you … inside of you..." He looked back up at me, his eyes worried. "I'm like a man possessed. I cannot get you out of my mind." His face reddened from the admission. "I want you. I want to make love to you. This does not feel like the 'me' that I know. It's making me crazy."

As I considered his words, I looked into his eyes and could see clearly who was speaking from behind those deep, dark brown orbs. It was all Albert. I moved towards him to gather him into my arms in a comforting hug but his words had changed the nature of my emotions. As he spoke, I could feel my energy flowing toward his, each of his words hitting my body like a tuning fork, until our vibrations were in perfect sync. And then, I understood.

"Oh, my," I said, nearly swooning from the weakness in my knees as I stood beside him. "This probably isn't good."

I sat down in the overstuffed chair across from the couch. It was hard to think about our spiritual mission, of working together, sharing our mediumship gifts, and teaching about life after death, when our bodies were suddenly so drawn to each other. The sensual feelings passing back and forth between us were completely different than those between Sebastian and I, where the attraction had sprung from a sudden understanding of our timeless connection and the raw sexual energy created by his fully masculine nature.

In Albert's case, it felt more magnetic. It was as if his body was pulling mine towards his, and it was almost irresistible. But while I knew I felt something deep for Albert, especially in light of the knowledge that we also shared lifetimes entwined, I knew that jumping right into a physical relationship with him, especially after having already had a sort of accidental

MICHELE DELUCA

sexual encounter, would disrupt the lovely relationship
we were building. Albert was an entirely different sort
than Sebastian. Just by knowing him the short time I
had, I understood he was contemplative and thought-
ful about each step he took in life.

I stood up and grabbed my coat. "Let's go for a
walk, Albert. We have to talk about this."

We walked through the village of Lily Dale, past
the colorful gardens and assorted styles of quaint sum-
merhouses. I usually loved walking down the streets
of the community, but this day we walked in silence
with our heads down, each of us waiting for the other
to begin. By the time we got to the lakefront beach,
I had formed a few thoughts. I just had to find the
right words. The day was windy and the temperatures
lower than normal for a Western New York summer,
so we had the beach to ourselves. The sand blew a
bit with a gentle wind, but the waves were placid and
hit the beach with soothing rolls. Overhead, seagulls
squawked and soared. It was a lovely day.

"First of all," I said, as we walked near the shoreline,
"I am so sorry about what happened when you came
back into your body and found that Sebastian and I
had been making love. If there was anything I could
do to change that memory, I would do it, because no
matter what you say, I will always feel we didn't quite
have your permission to use your body in that way." He
walked alongside me, silent, nodding. "Second," I continued, "between the three of us, we have discovered

something amazing, miraculous even, and I want to continue to work with you to explore the potentials of our connection." He turned to look at me with worry in his eyes. I could almost hear the word "but..." racing through his brain. I looked away, and continued walking as I considered how to broach the subject of our physical connection. He stayed with me, his long legs matching my deliberate strides through the sand. "Just so we're clear, I feel what you feel," I confessed.

He stopped in his tracks. I stood within a foot of him and felt the draw of his energy.

"You feel what I feel?" He shook his head. "Impossible."

I pointed my finger at his chest and then pointed back at my own chest. "Do you feel a pulling sensation here, between us? Right now?"

He nodded.

"And is the physical connection you're feeling almost impossible to resist?" His eyes looked deep into mine. The intimacy of his gaze was almost too much to bear. I withdrew my eyes, and turned toward the lake. "Me, too," I said. We were silent for a moment. Then I continued, "Is it fair to say that you feel some sort of love for me?"

He nodded again, closing his eyes.

"Well, I feel love for you, too," I admitted. "Perhaps it's because of the connection I was shown that exists between you and Sebastian and me over the course of lifetimes. We've been siblings, lovers, and parents to each other, as well as just friends and neighbors. We've explored so many aspects of human relationships between us. Which, from what I understand, is the way this earth experience is supposed to go."

"I'm not ready to have a relationship with you," he said. "It's too soon."

"I know," I said, presuming he meant that he was still longing for Julia.

I sighed, and sat down in the sand. He joined me, and we both stared out into the lake. After a moment, his brow furrowed. "Not just for me, but for you," he said. "I think your heart is still with Sebastian."

I sighed, and began absent-mindedly digging a little hole in the sand. "I agree. It's too soon."

Albert and I spent the afternoon at the beach, discussing the strange and unexpected turn our lives had taken, and then decided to simply go back to our separate lives for a time. Despite the physical and spiritual connection we were feeling toward each other, the events of the last few days had made us aware that moving too fast could be detrimental to any eventual relationship that might unfold between us. We would remain friends, support each other in our mediumship development, and work toward using our gifts to help others.

Later that night, in Maeve's class, we shared our experiences with our teacher and our fellow student, Tracy. We told them of our plan.

Tracy, who'd been enjoying every bit of our spiritual explorations, spoke straightforwardly with the aplomb of a young person: "What about the sexual attraction? What are you going to do about that?"

Albert reddened, and cleared his throat. We all looked at him. I wanted to hear his reply, too.

"Well…" He paused. "I'm not really used to discussing that sort of thing with women I'm not currently… in an intimate relationship with…but I certainly think that we need to control our impulses. They cannot control us."

We all nodded in seriousness, as if he had just recited a chemical formula. I hid a smile. I had already felt the extent of our physical attraction and while it wasn't as encompassing as what I'd felt with Sebastian, it was fascinating, nonetheless. After our adventures in the afterlife, I returned to my everyday existence with the surety that nothing happens without a reason and that even the worst possible scenarios have something to teach us. But what could sexual attraction have to do with spirituality? Why was I feeling such strong urges at this point in my life?

Certainly, my husband Michael and I had had a lovely sexual relationship in our early years together, but in our later years it had the energy of embers in a fireplace, burning hot only if we took the time to fan it. We didn't want to rip each other's clothes off when we passed each other in the hallway but some nights, lying next to each other in bed, our legs entwined, we came together with a depth of emotional connection that always surprised me with its strength. That was the reason his betrayal had knocked the life out of me and all the more reason I couldn't imagine jumping right into another intimate relationship. Sebastian had been a spiritual accident, as far as I was concerned. He had dropped into my life with the confounding familiarity of a long-lost love, and I had found his presence irresistible.

Now Sebastian was gone. It was probably best for both of us. A living person simply could not have an ongoing and intimate relationship with a dead man and that dead man could not grow in spirit if he was tethered to an earthbound soul. If I wanted what was best for both of us, I had to let him go.

It was different with Albert. There was no sense of urgency. I had learned that, like Sebastian, he had always been a part of my many lives and always would be. In what remained of this life, I was willing to let our relationship take its time to unfold, like the petals of a crocus pushing through snow, announcing the emergence of a sun-filled spring.

REBECCA'S EPILOGUE

Yesterday was my birthday. I am now officially ninety-seven years old. It was a lovely day. Several of my young teacher friends took me to lunch. I couldn't eat much, but I managed a glass of white wine, even though I knew it would keep me up all night. It was worth every delicious sip. At this point, nights and days are the same. If it's 3 a.m. and I can't sleep, I just put on a light and grab my notepad and scribble a few more lines of the book I'm working on. Or I forage for something wonderful from the fridge, like the sweet rice pudding that I buy from a Greek restaurant just down the highway from Lily Dale.

Time has fallen away and given me nothing but more time, with long days to ponder and imagine. I know that the end of my physical existence is near, but the greatest gift that Sebastian and Albert have given me is fearlessness totally unexpected from an old lady like me. And that's the joke, really. I don't feel old. Perhaps it's knowing what I know and my remarkable surety about having somewhere better to go, but I cannot even fathom a moment of uncertainty for what is to come. I feel like a young woman trapped inside an old woman's body, wanting to run and dance and play, but simply unable to summon the energy. It's not like I'm in bad shape for someone my age. I have kept fit with long daily walks and I am surprised at how well I've held up all these years. When I look into the mirror, an old lady looks back but she is someone who still loves and cares about the ways of the world.

I am, however, tired of being tired. I am unable to do much without paying for it with the aches and pains of bones and muscles that no longer move with agility. So I sit in Maeve's favorite chair, watching the birds swoop above the frozen lake in the morning mists of an icy February, enjoying the peace that overtakes Lily Dale during the winter months when most everybody flees to warmer climates. I used to head south in the winter too, when Albert and I were traveling around the country, lecturing about our experiences with Sebastian and promoting our books. Albert's gone now. I was at his side when he passed, and I'm not ashamed to admit I had to fight back feelings of jealousy. We both knew he would be with Julia and Sebastian once. Despite our many tender years together, I was glad for him.

I have known for some time that the heart expands with each opportunity to love. After my experiences with Sebastian in the afterlife, I came to understand that our time on earth is only about growing our ability to love. I know it sounds far too simple. Just love? How could that be? Why would someone create a whole world so its inhabitants could explore and enlighten themselves on matters of the heart? I don't know, but someone did.

After Sebastian, every person that came into my life pushed my heart open a little wider. As I looked forward, and backward in time, I realized that even my husband Michael, despite his betrayal, had taught me about love in its most important aspect: forgiveness. His redemption came to me through his child, created from the darkness of his adultery. I can still see her as when she first started spending summers with me, running into my classroom, her blue eyes dancing and her little hands reaching for mine, constantly reminding me that one can never predict when the darkness will lift to reveal a magnificent light.

Lillibeth. She was a remarkable child and though she didn't come through me, it appears that Michael's crazy idea of me helping to raise her was not so crazy after all. I have always felt as if a part of her belonged to me. It wasn't an easy relationship in the beginning. The first day her father brought her to me, in hopes that my work with children who have autism could help him reach her in some way, she screamed in fury and clutched the doorframe as if she was fighting for her life. But as soon as he put her down, she focused on something in the back of the room. It was a bookcase filled with children's books. Without a glance at me, she marched over to the case and stood in front of it. Her little body began to sway gently, forward and back, self-soothing. It reminded me of Charlie, the boy in my classroom so many years ago. Charlie had been the first to see Sebastian on the day that changed my life forever. He was the first child who helped me understand the fragile thread between autism and spirit. It didn't happen to all children diagnosed with autism, but it undeniably happened to some, and I had a feeling back then that Lillibeth was among those children for whom the human connection could be enhanced by a connection to the spirit world.

These children seemed to possess a variety of unusual gifts for healing touch and spirit communication, which their parents would ultimately recognize as something different from what little we knew back then about autism. Often, the families would find their way to our little summer seminars, where we tried to help the children make the connection between their unusual gifts and the world that Albert and I had explored. We would share stories about where we'd been and what it was like with Sebastian and Julia. To our surprise, many of the children had experienced similar encounters. Those who were able to communicate often recounted talking with spirits before they were born. They would tell stories of their birth and young lives as if they were visitors here, examining the odd ways of the culture they'd found. Our shared experiences gave the children and their families the certainty that every life had divine importance and meaning. It was satisfying and groundbreaking work, and by surprising coincidence, it changed the relationship between Michael and me, when I was able to help find the extraordinary gifts hidden behind his young daughter's aloof and explosive behavior.

And then, after several years, Sebastian returned. True to his word, he'd come back for Victoria when her disease finally took her, and we were all there waiting for him. Albert and I had created a family of sorts with Beth and Anne and Victoria. We saw them regularly over the next few years for delightful meals during which we'd share and speculate on our experiences of standing at the edge of forever. We watched as Victoria valiantly battled the cancer in her blood and while she occasionally visited the healers that would come to Lily Dale, partaking in sessions of Reiki, or other forms of energetic healing, she also employed the powerful chemicals of conventional medicine as I once had, in her attempt to stay alive and well. Sadly, the leukemia eventually had its way, but Victoria was graceful in accepting its victory, giving over her body but not her mind or spirit. The five of us would have long conversations about the irony of having evidence that life doesn't end with death and yet wishing death to stay as far away as possible from those that we love.

We'd been at Victoria's bedside for several days before she died, talking softly with Beth and Anne, and watching the room fill with occasional wisps of energy from those coming in from the afterlife to surround her with peace and comfort. We were waiting for Sebastian and he did not disappoint us. The last day of her life, I was sitting at Victoria's bedside. Beth and Anne had gone into the kitchen to make lunch for us, and Albert had gone into another room to take a phone call regarding a lecture he and I were planning that weekend. My eyes were closed. I was meditating in an effort to maintain the peacefulness in the room, concentrating on my breath as it moved in and out of my body. I felt him before I saw him. He came in with a gentle vibration I could feel and it was warm upon my flesh. I opened my eyes and the room seemed a little brighter, as if a ray of sunshine had burst through the curtained window. I looked into the corner of the room and though I couldn't see him there, he appeared clearly in my mind's eye as his elderly self, with wild white hair and the luminous dark eyes filled with love.

I glanced at the bed where Victoria slept, looking so thin and frail beneath the blanket. In the times we'd shared with her and Anne and Beth over the last two years, Albert and I had come to appreciate her humor and feisty spirit. I was filled with love for the woman and so grateful to be at her side to help her pass.

Then I heard Sebastian say to me, "Hello, Rebecca. It's almost time."

I nearly stopped breathing at the sound of his words in my head. He was there. Happiness filled me and I welcomed the forgotten feeling of wholeness that Sebastian brought to me. I couldn't see him but could surely feel him. "Hello, Sebastian," I said silently to the image in my head.

"I've missed you," he'd replied in a loving whisper, "but I am so proud of the work you and Albert are doing."

"Thank you," I responded, still not speaking aloud, but smiling. "You've been a big part of our success."

He was nodding in response when Anne came back with a tray of teacups. When she saw my eyes directed to the corner of the room, she froze so abruptly I heard the cups clatter on the tray.

"He's here, isn't he?" she asked.

"Yes, he's standing next to your mom's bed. He's waiting for her," I said.

Anne took in a breath. She placed the tray on an end table and sat at the foot of the bed, trying to see Sebastian. "I'm not ready for her to go."

"It's okay, sweetheart," I said, placing a hand on her knee. "It's not happening just now. Your father told us he would be here when your mom crossed over and he's just reminding us of that promise. We still have some time. I'm just not sure how much."

"Should I call someone from hospice?" she asked, anxiety in her voice. Victoria had been under hospice care for several days. The caregivers had made it clear that Anne and Beth should not be afraid to contact them if they needed help.

"No, dear. Your mother seems very comfortable, especially since your father arrived."

We returned our attention to Victoria, whose face had taken on a peacefulness I hadn't noticed before. Her lips were turned up slightly at the corners. I walked over to her bedside and brushed back some hair from her forehead. She didn't seem feverish or uncomfortable. "No, dear, I don't think we need to call them. I feel like she knows, somehow, that your dad is here with us."

Albert came into the room. By the resolute look on his face, I could see he also knew that Sebastian was there. "I felt him coming when I was in the car." He sat down in the chair next to mine as Anne handed him a cup of tea on a saucer. Then he sighed and leaned back in the chair. "He wants to talk to you and the girls."

Albert had always known that Sebastian would come back, as promised. When we talked about it, we discussed the possibility of Albert channeling Sebastian. It was a particularly challenging situation because in the years since we'd last seen Sebastian,

Albert and I had become lovers. We had both known it would happen, especially after I'd seen the painting Albert had created of me that day when I first walked into his home. The strokes of color on that canvas were as clear as sentences in a love letter. It was probably the most alluring sexual overture I'd ever experienced but I had been unable to consider it as such until Sebastian disappeared from our lives.

Once Albert and I started working together, writing and speaking about our experiences channeling Sebastian, we'd been invigorated by our shared passions for teaching and learning and it drew us even closer together. I came to appreciate the raise of his brow when he was considering a humorous or challenging thought that I'd put to him. His bark of laugher was the likely response to either. I came to see it as a sort of prize for rousing him spiritually and intellectually.

When we finally made love, it was precipitated by a moment when I was looking over his shoulder while he sat at his desk. He was rewriting a paragraph in the book we were working on. I had leaned over to point out a sentence on his computer that I thought could be stronger. I stopped mid-sentence, distracted, as he deliberately turned his head until his face was inches from my breast. He raised his eyes to meet mine and that was all it took. He stood, reached for my hand, and led me to his bedroom. What followed was the greatest lesson I ever learned about love. If you allow it, love will expand. There doesn't have to be just one great love. There can be two. There can be more. Love can encompass the whole world.

It didn't matter for a single second that our bodies were aging. Our spirits felt youthful and eternal and our lovemaking was more like a merging of souls than flesh. In the course of our union, I inhaled the musky scent of his skin and was able to sense the difference between making love to Sebastian and making love to Albert. The impossible connection I shared with Sebastian was like a nuclear explosion that smashed the whole world into dust. Making love with Albert was more like a single note from an orchestra that built to an all-consuming crescendo and brought tears to the eyes of the listener. Either way, the result was the same. I loved two men in a way I had never dreamed possible. It was as if my marriage to Michael had been a divine prelude to allow me to eventually understand the difference between relationships created within ordinary days and ones crafted from the awareness of eternity. And yet, between Albert and me, two expert communicators who loved nothing more than challenging each other, I could feel his unspoken uncertainty about the difference between making love with him and making love with Sebastian.

I assumed that Albert was afraid of the answer. I suppose I was, as well. So that day at Victoria's deathbed, Albert had to decide what to do. Could he deny Sebastian the opportunity to appear among us again?

Given that we both felt such an odd and compelling connection to our spirit friend, I knew he could not.

He'd sat up in his chair and turned to Anne, smiling resignedly. "I'm going to take off for a little bit and let your grandfather speak through me. Is that okay with you?"

She let out a breath. "Sure, that would be amazing."

He nodded and smiled weakly. "Yes, it would. I'm going to go into a meditation, and you can expect to see him shortly." Albert closed his eyes and began breathing deeply. We watched him for a few moments and in the silence of the room, I felt compelled to pray for divine support and guidance. I moved closer to the bed, speaking silently to my guides and angels, and placed a hand upon Victoria's as she lay, still and breathing shallowly.

Sebastian's voice called to us softly, "Hello, all my beloved ones."

He had come to us in a version of his older self, as was typical when he appeared for his daughter and grandchild. "Victoria is getting ready to leave with me," he said. He looked directly at Beth and spoke with gentle compassion. "I hope you are not afraid, little Bird."

Beth stood and rushed over to Sebastian, her words coming out in a sob of relief. "Pops," she said, "you're here!"

Sebastian held his arms open wide and Beth moved into his embrace. They stayed like that for a few moments and then he looked up at me over the top of her head. "Rebecca," he said, eyes blazing with vitality. "I'm so glad to see you."

"I'm glad you're here, as well," I replied, as our eyes met and locked. The look I saw there recalled every second of our time spent at the edge of eternity and in the private intimacy of our connection as he smiled gently and said simply, "I've missed you."

Then he turned to his daughter, sitting nearby, and reached for her hand. He raised it to his lips, kissing it sweetly. She touched his cheek and said softly, "Thank you for coming back for her."

She and her father turned their attention to Victoria, who appeared to struggle for each breath. "I'm so worried for her," Anne said. "It looks like she's in pain."

Sebastian touched Victoria's arm in a gentle caress and then turned again to Anne. "What's going to happen shortly is that your mom's spirit is going to leave with me, but she still has a few moments to hear your goodbyes. Once she completes the process, she will be momentarily confused. I'm hoping that when she sees me, she'll understand, and will come without fear to the most amazing place she's ever been."

Anne smiled. She trusted her father now, and so did I.

He hugged her, and then he walked over to me and pulled me up from my chair, wrapping his arms around me. He whispered in my ear, his breath impossibly sweet and warm. "All you have to do is call!"

Then, with our arms around each other, I felt his energy leave Albert's body. I had gotten quite expert at discerning the difference between the two energies. Sebastian's vibration was palpable and touching him was like putting your hand to a bridge as a train crosses over. Albert's energy was slower and warmer, like putting your hand into mittens that have been left near the fire.

Albert slowly returned. We exchanged a glance that said more than words could, about trust and love and a world without end. And then we turned and watched as Sebastian took Victoria's spirit home. On her last exhale, she opened her eyes wide, smiled at something we could not see and then was gone. I squinted and could just make out sparks of light from her escort, but I could see no other ethereal details of her departure.

Anne shut her eyes as tears slipped down her cheeks. Her hands were folded in prayer. Beth reached for her grandmother's lifeless hand and caressed it. My heart ached for them both. I was about the same age as Beth when I lost my own mother and grandmother and I could clearly recall the overwhelming feelings of grief. But at such times, there is nothing else to do except sit and be present with the sadness. So Albert and I sat with Beth and Anne until the hospice workers came to help prepare Victoria's body for the funeral director, whose dark hearse pulled up silently into the driveway. Anne and Beth dressed Victoria in her favorite light blue dress and Beth combed her hair in place. There was a vase of wildflowers on the kitchen table, and Beth dried their stems and placed them in her mother's hands.

We sent her off with her favorite book of poems from Kahlil Gibran, opened to the page with his poem about death: "And when the earth shall claim your limbs, then shall you truly dance." Anne placed the book on her chest, beneath the flowers and bent over to kiss her forehead. While I understood the grief that Anne and Beth would struggle with, I felt pleased for Victoria's gentle release to eternity and to know that all was well between her and Sebastian.

Though he had said he would not return to this world until he came back for me on the last days of my life, something shifted that day in the relationship he shared with Albert and me. He made it clear he knew my relationship with Albert was the backbone for our work ahead, and he gave us space for love to bloom as we worked to change the lives of children and families who lived with autism. But, every now and then, Sebastian would return to the classroom. There, channeled through an eventually obliging Albert, he was his jovial self, and the children responded to his playful spirit the way most everyone else did. He helped them understand many things, and it was satisfying to watch him come through Albert and interact with the children in a manner no living human seemed able to. I would often sit in the back of the room in a rocking chair, smiling as I listened to him answer their questions.

"Do you ever see God?" the young ones asked him, again and again. He would always reply the same way, pointing at the questioner and replying, "Yes, I see him much the same way that you can, which is everywhere. I see him in the sunshine and the flowers, I feel him in the wind. He's in everything, including you and me. His energy is within us all," he would say. It was the same thing kids have been told in churches around the world since forever, but having been to the beyond with Sebastian and Albert, I knew that his words were absolutely true.

My idea to create the school had been sparked a long time ago, that first day I'd encountered Sebastian in my classroom, and my student, Charlie, had been so entranced by his energy. It was the same with so many children diagnosed with autism who found their way to us. Although some were very high functioning, others would never quite focus until Albert channeled Sebastian, and then suddenly, their attention was rapt. They would sit and interact with him for hours, some just watching intently, others chattering away, often revealing just how much they actually understood. Typically, by the end of the summer, each child seemed more engaged with their families and the world and more content in their lives. The work was deeply satisfying and provided a level of success we couldn't have reached without Sebastian.

One night, after the children had gone for the day, Albert and I were on the porch of Maeve's lake house, sipping our tea. I held my breath for a moment so I could hear the soft sounds of waves moving to shore from the lake nearby. "Do you miss him?" he asked.

I smiled before I answered. I knew who he meant, but was quiet as I gathered my thoughts. "No, I don't," I admitted honestly. "The people I miss are those I don't feel every day. I miss my mother. I would give anything for a few more minutes with her, so I could tell her she was right about Michael and apologize for my unkind words; and I could tell her about you and Sebastian."

He was quiet as I continued. " I miss Maeve, my teacher, my friend, who was always there for me. I haven't been able to connect with her either, and I always hoped that once she passed, she could help me connect with my mother. Then I feel guilty, because after all she's given to us, how could I expect more from her?"

Every moment we spent on that porch, I felt gratitude toward Maeve, who had left me her Lily Dale lake house in her will because her own daughters had no interest in the place. I had been at her side with them during her passing when Maeve was in her late nineties, as I am now, and it filled my heart to see how lightly we can leave our bodies if we don't cling to the idea of staying in them.

Albert looked out toward the lake. The moon was full, and shone down upon the water like a great spotlight directed our way. "It's hard to believe we're in our seventies now," he'd told me that night. "I never expected to enjoy..." he cleared his throat, "the...physical pleasures of our relationship at this age. It makes me wonder. Do you ever miss him in *that* way."

I nodded, without looking at him, so he couldn't see the smile in my eyes. Discovering in my senior years that making love to Albert was still the ultimate expression of the love between us, surprised me. It was amazing what having passion for life can do for the retention of vigor and optimism.

Perhaps that was another reason we were still so attracted to each other, Albert and I, because we so adored the lives we had created for ourselves together; yet I understood the line of questioning that night on the porch. As much as he was seeking to affirm that I would love him to the end of time, I could feel that he was trying to find his place in the triad that was the greatest gift in our lives, and where Sebastian was an equal partner. But did I miss Sebastian in *that* way? I examined my thoughts and chose my words carefully, so he would never need to ask again.

"Albert, there is no comparison between you and Sebastian," I said. "He is a spirit, living somewhere we can't easily go, and you are a living, breathing man, made from human flesh." I sighed. "Sebastian is...like an angel. He has been the key to our work, proving to us that there is a divine plan, and that when we leave this life, there is something more wonderful waiting. Yes, I love him. I think you do, too. But in the same way that you can continue to love Julia, and still love me so very much, that is the way I love you, right here and right now."

A boyish smile of relief overtook his face, as if this was comforting news. Then he took my hand. I tried to hold the feel of his hand in mine as a precious memory. We both knew that the time we had left in our aging bodies was limited. It wasn't long after that when Albert received the diagnosis of the heart condition that would end his physical life. I was getting used to sitting at deathbeds by then, but no matter how aware one is of the outcome, there is still the worry of a smooth passage and the sadness over the giant, empty space left by a departed loved one. It was harder to say goodbye to Albert than it was to Sebastian. He grounded my world with his calm, wise demeanor and his daily efforts to add simple comforts to my life.

I would so miss how he always brought me coffee when I sat at my desk and worked on our books. I'd look up at him, my glasses perched on my nose, and he would nod approvingly and ask, "How did I get so lucky?" I would reply, "We are blessed, my husband."

Near his death, when he was unable to make love to me, we would simply lie in bed with our hands clasped. When he was no longer able to reach for me, I would sit next to the bed and place my hand on his heart, glad that I could still feel him. But as the thumping got softer, I knew it would soon be Albert's time to leave, and I was not ready for him to go. My reluctance to release him made for a challenging death experience, and yet I could not help myself. The idea of his death made my heart clench tight. After all the years that had passed, I fell back upon the dark thoughts of abandonment that had plagued me when I lost my mother and grandmother and later, Michael. Even in that returned darkness, it struck me as odd that I did not feel abandoned by Sebastian. I knew he was always there. I could feel him whenever I needed to.

Thank God for Lillibeth. She has been at my side like a silent avenger, bound to me through a maternal link that connects us as tightly as the genetic ties from which she was born. She moved into the lake house with me, leaving vacant the home Michael and her mother left her when they moved south for warmer climates. She is nearly fifty-years-old now, but the years have been kind to my little girl, the daughter of my soul.

Once she came to me in my classroom, we were able to bond through our love of reading. Though she never spoke, I talked to her endlessly as we sat next to each other in a pair of old rocking chairs. Eventually, she would sit with me, bringing her favorite *Pat the Bunny* book, which she would tap with her dimpled little hand when she wanted me to open the cover so she could feel the different textures as I read. I was surprised when she indicated an interest in young adult fiction. I read her all of the Harry Potter books and a variety of stories with characters that had super powers and used those powers to make their worlds a better place.

One day, when she was about eight, I came into my classroom expecting to find her, and the room was empty. I panicked. She was supposed to be there with Albert and several other students. Then I heard the tapping.

I went into Maeve's old reading room, which I had left untouched, and there sat Lillibeth in front of an old typewriter, tapping away at the keys. Albert and several of the children were gathered behind her, transfixed. When I walked over, I could see that the ribbon was just barely making an imprint on the paper that she had somehow managed to slip into the roll. Lillibeth was typing happily, her eyes fixed on the pages, a look of absolute peace on her face. Albert saw me at the door and motioned for me to come inside. He pointed to the words on the page. My silent, beautiful Lillibeth was communicating. Her fingers tapped away at the keyboard and the words just kept coming. Clearly, she had been waiting a long time to be able to share what was on her mind. And my little Lillibeth had a lot to say.

LILLIBETH'S EPILOGUE

My name is Lillibeth St. Claire. I was Rebecca's student and she was very wonderful to me. Rebecca is gone now and I am sometimes sad to be without her. But sitting at her bedside when she died showed me that everything she taught me was true.

I have been at many deathbeds since then. People call me a death doula, maybe because they can find no other name to describe what I do. Instead of welcoming babies into the world, like midwives and birthing doulas usually do, I help people's spirits leave this world. Rebecca taught me how to do that.

It's only death, after all, and since Rebecca and Albert and Sebastian have taught me that no one ever really dies, I've never been afraid. How can I be afraid when I am able to see beautiful light move out of a sick or old body like it's stepping out of a wet bathing suit? Most people can't see what I see. They just think their dying person is leaving them forever and it makes them really sad. But sometimes, I can help make things a little bit better.

My first death experience was the day Albert died. I was thirty-five years old then, and had spent years learning from Rebecca and Albert. My parents let me spend every summer with my father's ex-wife and the professor, after they saw the progress I was making at their school. I was at Rebecca's house when I found the old typewriter on the bookshelf. Every time I would tap out words that had been stored in my brain, it felt like a cocoon had cracked open, and little butterflies were released. I still have every page I've ever written, starting with that first day. I've placed them in binders so I can take them out and read them whenever I want to. The pages begin with my first compositions, with the words "water nice me play" or "me see elephant book." As I got older and my grammar improved, I was able to express myself more clearly. This is from one of my entries as a twelve-year-old: "I will be walking by the lake today as I need to find more of those pretty purple stones for my collection."

The typewriter made me feel very happy for a long time. Then my parents bought me a computer tablet, which gave me the ability to speak through a digital soundboard, but I rarely used the board because the voice coming out of the program didn't sound anything like the voice I heard in my head. To me, it was like the difference between the fancy writing on a wedding invitation and the fat lines of a felt marker. I always preferred the typewriter. That old, black Underwood helped people see what I wanted to say.

I wrote a lot about the day I sat at Albert's death-bed. I was very sad. Rebecca was the only other person in the room when I entered and sat by her side. I had never seen someone die and I was afraid Albert's passing would be horrible. But Rebecca had asked me to be present, and so I wanted to be there

As I sat beside Albert, he looked like he was sleeping.

Then, I saw Rebecca look up at a corner of the room near the ceiling. "They're here," she told me in a quiet voice. "They've been waiting for him. There's Sebastian," she smiled, pointing to something I couldn't see. I have always felt happy when Sebastian was near. I was glad he was in the room with us. She paused as if listening. "I know," she said to someone I could not see. "I am so glad." Then she turned to me. "Julia is here now, too," she told me. "Thank Heaven." She smoothed a crease on Albert's forehead. "They're here for you. You should go now, my darling. I'll be okay."

I peered up into the corner. I could see nothing but the yellow walls and white ceiling. I looked at her and I shook my head. I couldn't see them.

She smiled. "Close your eyes, child. Take a deep breath and relax. Even if you can't see them, you may be able to feel them."

I shut my eyes, and breathed out all the bad feelings I felt about Albert's leaving. That's when I saw them behind my eyelids, and they looked like angels stepping out of the darkness. I saw Sebastian in the place that Rebecca told me is called my mind's eye. He was as Rebecca had always described. Crisp white shirt, thick black hair. He was with a blonde woman who was smiling. I guessed that she was Albert's first wife, Julia.

Albert's eyes fluttered, his breathing slowed and then his life left his body with a puff of his last breath. He was gone. I looked over at Rebecca.

"Did you see that?" she asked me. "Did you see his energy lift from his body? Rebecca smiled and shut her eyes, holding Albert's hand. I counted four minutes before she spoke. "He's with Julia and Sebastian now. He will be fine." And that was that.

For many days after Albert died, I was very sad. I liked spending time with the professor and hearing his stories about the afterlife. Rebecca was less sad than me. I watched as she met with clients, worked with the children, and continued to write her books. She didn't seem to miss Albert at all. When I asked her, she smiled and told me that he hadn't left her and that they had conversations every single day about his new experiences in the next world. She hugged me and told me that Albert's death was proof of everything she had hoped was true. We never died. And that was that.

She told me then that my being at Albert's death-bed had helped her to see something special in me. She said it was because my brain presented information to me in images, it seemed easier for me to get information from those who were dead and trying to communicate with the living. She wanted to begin nurturing my gifts and teaching me how to understand what I saw.

After that, Rebecca sought out those who were near the end of their lives, and we would offer to help the person and their family get ready.

Rebecca was the one who told me that death is much like birth, only opposite. She said birth could sometimes be a messy, painful, experience. Death is the same, only backwards. She told me that when death came at the end of a good life, it could be beautiful. She was right. Her death was beautiful.

We were in her study. She was moving slowly, trying to find a book for me from the shelves. Suddenly, she put a hand up to her forehead.

"Oh, my," she said, "I'd better sit down." She grabbed the back of the cushioned char and sat. I rushed to her side and helped her lean her head against the fabric.

"He's coming," she whispered. "My heart is beating so fast. I can feel the vibration of my body increasing. It feels quite wonderful." She turned her eyes up and smiled. "Look."

For the first time, I could see them; so many that the room seemed filled. I could see Albert, and Maeve, and others I didn't recognize. They were misty, shining bodies of light. As I took in every face, each one seemed so happy, that I could not be afraid.

Rebecca gasped. "Mama?" Tears filled her eyes. "Mama, you're here! I've missed you so much."

She tried to sit up, but fell back against the arm of the chair. "My mother is here," she said to me, "and my grandmother. This is amazing, and look there… Maeve," she whispered, putting her hand to her heart. "They're all here for me, but…"

I saw Sebastian move to the front of the group. Beside him stood another body made of light. It was Albert.

"They're all here," she whispered.

Sebastian and Albert each reached a hand for her. My heart started beating faster. I realized they were taking her, and I became afraid. I grabbed her hand. "Wait," I shouted, "Rebecca, you can't leave me! I'll be all alone."

She turned her head to look at me. "Lillibeth, you spoke!" She smiled a little smile, like she was falling asleep. "That's amazing."

I put my hand to my throat. "I…I did."

I suddenly felt dizzy. I closed my eyes and Rebecca put her hand upon mine. Pictures began flashing through my head. I saw me working as medium on the Assembly Hall stage. Then, I saw a man. I couldn't make out his face, but I knew that he would be my husband, and I felt that he would love me and I would love him. I saw myself teaching in Rebecca's classroom, with small children like I once was, and they were beaming light, like the spirits that filled the room. I saw myself at many different deathbeds, sitting with the dying, and helping them into the arms of their loved ones in spirit.

Then the images disappeared like someone had shut off a television. But everything I saw that day was something I would never forget. I was shown the life I would have, even though Rebecca was leaving me. I sat up straight and decided to begin that life. If anyone was going to help Rebecca out of this, it was going to be me, and that was that. But what was I to do? She had told me once that all I needed was be peaceful and unafraid. And so I was.

I did not want her to go. She had been telling me for years that I was one of the greatest gifts in her life. I hadn't been born from her, but she said my father had gotten his wish, and he and my mother and Rebecca had raised me together. Although I loved my parents, it was with Rebecca, at her little house in Lily Dale, where I felt safe and happy.

I stared into her wide eyes as they filled with tears, though she was smiling. She turned her head to me a final time and whispered, "I love you, Lillibeth. We will meet again, when it is time."

"I love you, too," I said, my new voice sounding odd and foreign, like croaking from the frogs at the lake. Rebecca slowly closed her eyes for the last time. I put my head upon her chest to see if there was any sound coming from her heart.

It was then I heard the music. I wasn't certain at first that it was music at all, but just a buzzing in my ear. I didn't know it then, but Rebecca's leaving, though it only took minutes, was the longest, look into the beyond that I would ever again have at the bedside of a dying person.

A vapor rose from Rebecca's body. As I watched in awe, everything about her that was alive, that made her who she was, lifted out of her body. I could see right through her as she moved towards Sebastian, and their two spirits embraced in a swirl of energy. Then Albert moved toward Rebecca and Sebastian, and he wrapped them both within his arms.

I watched as hard as I could. The light in the room seemed to darken, and suddenly I was alone with Rebecca's body. I walked to her bedside and kissed her forehead, then I stared at what was left of her. I knew it was my job to see to what remained. And that was that.

I had spent many hours sitting with those who were dying and I still didn't know where they all went, but when Rebecca died, I got a peek through an open door just before it closed and I would spend the rest of my life trying to get a better look.

I pulled the blankets around Rebecca's body and lit a violet candle on the bedside table. The flame gave the room a lavender scent and, from that day on whenever Rebecca was with me in spirit, the air around me would smell as if someone had brought the dried herb into the room.

I lifted my cell phone and texted the reverend from the Spiritualist church nearby.

As I waited for him to arrive, I sat quietly in the room with death. When Rebecca and I began our work together, I had thought of death as this giant beast that hollered and roared. If I tried not to be afraid as I sat beside the person who was leaving, the beast would calm down and sit beside me. Then we would wait together for the door to open to eternity. Death scared me less with each visit, but there was still so much I didn't understand, like why death stole young and old like it didn't matter who was who. Why sometimes it was so easy, and sometimes it was so hard to go through that door?

I would spend the rest of my life trying to figure it out. I wanted to learn as much as I could so I could tell people, so they would not be so afraid. And so, I have.

If you ask me, death is really not the end at all, but the start of a life as new and happy as when a baby is born. That baby might cry upon arrival, because someone has just yanked it from a warm and quiet place. But, all that scariness goes away when the child is put into its momma's arms, and feels quiet and safe once more. Then, their new adventure begins. Dying is like that, only way better.

I see what happens. That's my gift. I get to watch as people are birthed into death and go off to a place so filled with happiness that I have no words to describe it. People sometimes say I couldn't possibly see what I see, but why would I make anything up? For me, there are no better stories than the ones that really happen.

There will always more. Forever more. And that is that.

A NOTE FROM THE AUTHOR, MICHELE DELUCA

Since I was a young woman, I have been obsessed with finding out why we are given life, and why life must end with death. As a journalist, I've only known one way to find the answers I sought. I began to read.

Several decades ago, as a new mother, I started my quest for understanding with a book called "Seat of the Soul," by Gary Zukav, given to me by a friend. I read it six times over the course of the next few years, because I could not believe Zukav's certainty that we are all more than we currently understand. Around the same time, I found Dr. Bernie Siegel's "Peace Love and Healing," and Carolyn Myss' books on her work as a medical intuitive and later her books on spiritual archetypes. Then, there was Dr. Brian Weiss's books on reincarnation and Dr. Raymond Moody's research on contacting the dead.

For thirty years, I have always tried to have a new book in progress, by a wide variety of authors on such subjects, because I have found hope in the true stories and research about what comes after. The stories help me to move through this life empowered, hope-filled and without fear.

I have been particularly fascinated by books on channeling, because I wonder where the wisdom comes from. I started with the volumes of the "Seth Material," by Jane Roberts. I've also read many books about Edgar Cayce, the channeler from Virginia Beach, who received healing information each day as he reclined for an afternoon rest. They called him "The Sleeping Prophet," and built a center in Virginia Beach to house the information he channeled, so it would be available for generations to come.

My favorite channeler is Esther Hicks, who for many years has traveled the world to share the wisdom she channels from a collective of funny and brilliant otherworld guides who call themselves by the singular name of Abraham. The Abraham-Hicks books and YouTube videos have brightened so many of my days with their thoughts on how to proceed with peace and joy through this complicated, crazy and often frightening world. I am profoundly grateful to Esther and her now-deceased husband, Jerry, who have so generously allowed sessions with the spiritual collective to be shared free on YouTube, and who continue their loving work together, though Jerry is in another place.

Beyond channeling, I have collected hundreds of stories related by people who have had "out of body," or "near death experiences." Those stories have convinced me we do not really ever die, and that conviction has led me to reexamine with intensity, all the ways we humans live, love and heal.

Science has proved that we are made of energy. Researchers are now starting to agree with contemporary intuitives and the spiritual guidance that indicates our outlook influences our energetic vibration, which impacts our health and the quality of our existence.

As such, I believe, the task of each lifetime is to find love and joy in all we do, as that appears to be the pathway to raising our vibration. We can tune in to those feelings through prayer, meditation and play; or by simply finding activities that make us happy.

I believe we must commit to these tasks as if our lives depend on it, because the success of our lives, our satisfaction and happiness, truly does depend on it.

And then, when we leave this life, I believe that our energy moves out of the human body and returns to the great beyond, more vibrant and alive than it is possible to imagine.

It doesn't matter what religion you follow — so many stories affirm what the sages have said since time began: There are many pathways to God and to those waiting for us in the beyond. We are told they love us equally and unconditionally, no matter what. That's what I have read and heard in the hundreds of reports

I've encountered that people have shared about their "near death experiences," each story unique but impossibly similar. All who have experienced such revelations can't be making it up, nor can they be imagining the way their lives are profoundly changed after such experiences occur.

As a journalist, my work is based upon the stories people tell me and what they believe is their truth. In the newsroom, I collect those stories and words and share them as part of the news of the day. But, at the end of the day, I believe the life-changing stories told by those who have come back from the beyond are the most important news to be shared. Such stories bring us understanding, peace, and a reason to be hopeful, forevermore.

If you have a story to share that you believe will help others live more fully and heal more completely, I would be honored to hear it and to share it. You can email me at mcdeluca@aol.com or contact me through my Facebook page, "Forever More: A Love Story from the Edge of Eternity." If you are moved to share your thoughts about this book, consider placing a review on Amazon.com to help others decide whether this story is one they might like to read. You can also visit my blog and read some of my other work at www.micheledeluca.net.

In the end, I wish you Godspeed to your beautiful destiny. All the evidence I have points the way towards forever, where there will always be more gifts to come for each of us. Forever, there will be more waiting. I will see you there.

Michele DeLuca

CPSIA information can be obtained at www.ICGtesting.com
Printed in the USA
BVOW01s0221230816

459875BV00019B/101/P